The Laurel Shakespeare

Each play is presented in a separate volume handsomely designed to incorporate these special features:

THE TEXT is a modern restoration of the original folios completed in 1965 by *Charles Jasper Sisson*.

THE FORMAT designed for this volume employs the largest and most readable type available in any popular edition of the plays.

THE MODERN COMMENTARY by actors, directors and critics recently associated with the respective plays offer an authoritative insight into a special aspect of the play. Charles Jasper Sisson is acknowledged to have been one of the world's greatest living authorities on Elizabethan life and thought in general and on Shakespeare in particular. At the time of his death in 1966, he was Senior Fellow at the Shakespeare Institute, Stratford-upon-Avon.

THE INTRODUCTION by the General Editor, *Francis Fergusson*, University Professor of Comparative Literature at Rutgers, provides dramatic and critical background.

SHAKESPEARE AND HIS THEATRE, also by *Professor Fergusson*, presents the known facts of Shakespeare's life and dramatic career along with a description of the Globe company.

THE GLOSSARY NOTES, especially prepared for this volume by Lawrence Blonquist, Rutgers University, define Elizabethan terms and special allusions not found in desk dictionaries.

The Laurel Shakespeare
Francis Fergusson, General Editor

Henry the Eighth

by William Shakespeare

Text edited by Charles Jasper Sisson

Commentary by Charles Jasper Sisson

Published by
DELL PUBLISHING CO., INC.
750 Third Avenue, New York, N.Y. 10017
Bibliographies and "Shakespeare and His Theatre"
and Introduction
Copyright © 1958, 1968 by Francis Fergusson
Copyright ©, 1968 by Dell Publishing Co., Inc.
All rights reserved
Laurel ® TM 674623, Dell Publishing Co., Inc.
Text of the play reprinted by permission of
Harper and Row, New York, N.Y.
Frontispiece drawings by Paul Wenck after
the Droeshout engraving in the First Folio
First printing—November 1968
Printed in U.S.A.

Contents

Introduction BY FRANCIS FERGUSSON	7
Suggestions for further reading	14
A note on the text	14
Commentary BY CHARLES J. SISSON	16
HENRY VIII	29
Shakespeare and His Theatre BY FRANCIS FERGUSSON	192
Suggestions for further reading	212
Glossary BY LAWRENCE BLONQUIST	219
Note on the General Editor	223
Note on the Type and Layout	223

Introduction by the General Editor

This play was almost certainly written in 1613, two years after *The Tempest,* which would make it the very last play Shakespeare wrote. Many critics during the last hundred years have questioned Shakespeare's authorship of it, rightly pointing out that its tone is different from the rest of his work. But Heminge and Condell, Shakespeare's lifelong associates and the publishers of the First Folio, attributed it all to him, and most experts are now inclined, for lack of any compelling evidence to the contrary, to accept their authority. Professor Sisson has explained all this in his illuminating account of the play's varying critical reception since its first appearance three hundred and fifty years ago (page 16). And he, too, lent his authority to the view that the play is essentially Shakespeare's.

It was probably written on the occasion of the visit of the Elector Palatine, who was in England to celebrate his marriage to James I's daughter Elizabeth. This important state occasion, especially since it involved another Elizabeth, would explain why Shakespeare felt obliged to return to the theatre after the "farewell" of *The Tempest.* It might also help one to understand the play's rather pedestrian quality—for it lacks the poetic inspiration, not only in language but in characterization and in the conception of the whole, which one expects to find in Shakespeare. It is not to be compared with the masterpieces; yet it is competent and stageworthy, just as one would expect the work of an "old professional" like Shakespeare to be: he met his assignment "as our Roman actors do,/ With untired spirits and formal constancy" (*Julius Caesar* II, i, ll. 226–227).

For the events of Henry's reign pictured in the play Shakespeare relied, as usual, upon the Chroniclers, Holinshed and Hall, and (for Cranmer's story, the main matter of Act V) upon Foxe's *Actes and Monuments of Martyrs*. He altered the chronology when it suited his purpose, but except for that he followed his sources closely, often using their very language with only such slight changes as were required to turn the prose into blank verse. The events he chose to represent would have been familiar to his audience (who might have heard about them from their own fathers or grandfathers) and he calls attention to their authenticity in the Prologue: "Think ye see/ The very persons of our noble story,/ As they were living." Shakespeare's audience loved to see "the very persons" of legend or history walking and talking on the stage.

The play begins with an eyewitness account of the famous "Field of the Cloth of Gold" when Henry, as a young king, met the young king of France, François I, with a great display of emulous splendor; and it ends with the auspicious christening of the infant Elizabeth. It is hardly a play in the usual sense of the word, but rather a series of loosely interwoven stories of some of the strong personalities that rose and fell, in the ceaseless power struggles of the court, during that part of Henry's reign. In the course of the first three acts we see Cardinal Wolsey reach the height of his power and prestige, and then fall in a moment when Henry discovers his secret correspondence with the Pope. Wolsey's machinations include his skillful ruin of his enemy, the Duke of Buckingham, and his careful promotion of Henry's divorce from his first wife, Katherine of Aragon. That divorce —Henry's first and most painful—enabled him to marry Anne Bullen, who was destined to become the mother of the great Elizabeth, as everyone in the audience knew. Ceremonious pageants and processions (staged as nearly as possible just as they had been originally) are a very important part of this play, and the fourth act consists entirely of two contrasting pageants: the elaborate procession celebrating Anne's coronation, and the pious death of Queen Katherine, with a ballet of white-robed figures that represent her vision of her reception into heaven. The fifth act is devoted largely to the rise of Cranmer, the Protestant churchman whom Henry made Archbishop of Canterbury after Wolsey's fall. Cranmer gives a prophetic eulogy of the infant Elizabeth at the christening ceremony that ends the play, and adds, for good measure, a prophecy of the felicitous reign of James I, who was, of course, on the throne when the play was first performed.

The stories of Wolsey and Buckingham, of Queen Katherine and Anne Bullen, and of Cranmer, as Henry protects him from his enemies and then makes him the head of the English Church, are fast-moving and easy to follow, but the meaning Shakespeare saw in them, and, in general, his purpose and attitude in writing this play, are still in dispute. *Henry VIII* superficially resembles the earlier History Plays in its appeal to the audience's patriotism and in its assumption that the national welfare depends upon the Crown. But the Crown is never in serious jeopardy, as it is in the plays about the Wars of the Roses, and there is no significant central conflict as there is in all the better Histories and Tragedies. It is true that Henry grows in personal freedom and power as he gets rid of the formidable Wolsey, divorces Katherine to marry young Anne, defies Rome, and makes his loyal servant Cranmer archbishop; but these successful moves, which cost the king very little, are hardly the result of any consistent or conscious policy on his part. His wives and his courtiers have clearer and stronger motives, and more interesting careers, than the king. We watch their rises and falls with the comfortable sense that the body politic is secure, much as we now cozily read about the careers of movie stars and the doings of the royal family.

It is often said that the play falls apart at Act IV, when Wolsey's story is over, and Cranmer's, which fills Act V, has not yet begun; and it is sometimes concluded, from this looseness of structure, that Shakespeare cannot have been responsible for the design of the play as a whole. But he employed a similar episodic structure in the late romances, especially *Pericles* and *Cymbeline*, which also lack a single central conflict with a clear climax and turning point. In such plays, Shakespeare is less interested in the success or failure of conscious human effort than he is in the "divinity that shapes our ends,/ Rough-hew them how we will," as Hamlet puts it. The Prologue of *Henry VIII* calls our attention to the common mortal fate that inevitably overtakes Henry's famous courtiers:

>   Think you see them great,
> And followed with the general throng and sweat
> Of thousand friends. Then, in a moment, see
> How soon this mightiness meets misery.

We are expected to watch the predestined course of events with detachment, and from that point of view above the battle—or subsequent to it—neither the moral qualities of individuals nor the immediate political issues seem very important.

That may be one reason why Shakespeare leaves unanswered a number of questions about the events of the play which seem important to us, if we are trying to judge the rights and wrongs of Henry's reign. What, for instance, was the king's real motive in divorcing Katherine? Was he really troubled, as he insists, about the legality of his marriage to his brother's widow? Or did he simply want to marry Anne? Or was he, like many another passionate man, "sincerely" deluding himself with his belated qualms of conscience (II, ii and iv)? Perhaps the whole matter was too awkward for Shakespeare to handle frankly on the occasion of another royal marriage; but when a dramatist refrains from looking into his characters' hearts, he forfeits the immediate sense of life. In the great plays the characters are vivid and convincing because Shakespeare has his eye on their true springs of action; in this play he shows little interest in motive in that intimate sense. The fact that Anne would give birth to the great Elizabeth was, from the point of view adopted in this play, much more significant than the actual cause of the cruel divorce that made the happy event possible.

Unresolved problems of motivation also surround the stories of Wolsey and Buckingham. Was Buckingham really guilty of treason, as the king seems to believe when he allows him to be executed? Or was he the straightforward, gruffly honest type he seems when we first meet him, an innocent victim of Wolsey's skillful machinations? We hear him protest his innocence and forgive everyone on his way to his execution, but the First and Second Gentlemen who discuss the case, though they like and pity him, seem unsure whether he is innocent or not. As for Cardinal Wolsey, we see unmistakably that he is cruel, ruthless and unscrupulous as he destroys his enemies and builds his own wealth and power; but he, too, suddenly makes a pious end when the king cuts him down, assuring us that he repents his life of worldly greed and now craves only forgiveness all around and the peace of heaven. Of course, there are plenty of characters in Shakespeare who are not what they seem, and plenty who have a change of heart when their battles are ended. What makes this play unusual is not the complex tangle of good and evil in the characters, but the fact that we see their contradictory acts only from a distance, without being sure what makes them, just as the two Gentlemen do in their scene with Buckingham.

The portrait of Queen Katherine is strikingly different from that of the other important characters, for her motives, as she endeavors to surmount her unjust rejection with dignity, are perfectly clear. The majority of critics find Katherine the most credible and sympathetic character in the play. Perhaps that is because the personality of the real Katherine is so strongly felt in the Chronicles which Shakespeare closely followed. She comes through as Spanish in her complete, dignified acceptance of the woman's role, no matter how meanly the king and his ecclesiastical advisers treat her. When she is robbed of her whole status as wife, mother and queen, instead of receiving the ceremonious respect traditionally accorded a Spanish matriarch, our sympathy is all with her, and our enthusiasm for Henry's marriage to Anne is correspondingly dampened. Thus, the vitality of Katherine's role raises the question of how Shakespeare wanted us to feel about Henry's divorce and remarriage. Did he expect us to relish the irony of the story—the fact that such shabby dealing led to so happy a result, the birth of the miraculous Elizabeth herself? Was he showing us once more that God works in mysterious ways? Or did he assume that his audience, stimulated by the festivities of the royal marriage and impatiently waiting for the birth of the great queen, was in no mood to worry about moral problems?

I think one may find a clue to Shakespeare's own view of the ruthless game of court life in the scene (II, iii) between Anne Bullen and the Old Lady, which he must have devised himself without the help of his sources. Anne and the Old Lady have just learned that Katherine is to be divorced; they agree that she does not deserve such treatment and that in general it would be better to accept a lowly status than to fall from a high one:

OLD LADY
                    Alas poor lady,
She's a stranger now again.

ANNE
                    So much the more
Must pity drop upon her. Verily
I swear, 'tis better to be lowly born,
And range with humble livers in content,
Than to be perked up in a glistering grief,
And wear a golden sorrow.

OLD LADY
                    Our content
Is our best having.

But then Anne (who guesses Henry's infatuation with her) insists that she would not be a queen if she could; and the Old Lady, who has lived all her life at court, grows mocking:

'Tis strange; a threepence bowed would hire me,
Old as I am, to queen it. But I pray you,
What think you of a duchess? Have you limbs
To bear that load of title?

by the General Editor

The Lord Chamberlain comes to announce to Anne that Henry has made her Marchioness of Pembroke, with an income of a thousand pounds a year; and the Old Lady is inspired to even more sardonic mirth:

> By this time
> I know your back will bear a duchess. Say,
> Are you not stronger than you were?

The unjust ups and downs of life at court are seen with devastating clarity, but they are accepted as inevitable, greedy human nature being what it is. The Old Lady sees the worldly game, even while she is in it, with the objectivity that Buckingham and Wolsey reach only when they are ready to die. Old Lear, at the end of his life, has the same vision of the bitter struggles of ambitious men, but he expresses it in such poetry as is not to be found anywhere in this play:

> So we'll live,
> And pray, and sing, and tell old tales, and laugh
> At gilded butterflies; and hear poor rogues
> Talk of court news, and we'll talk with them too,
> Who loses, and who wins, who's in who's out;
> And take upon's the mystery of things,
> As if we were God's spies. [*King Lear,* V, iii, 11-17]

In *Henry VIII* we follow court news and learn who's in, who's out, but the deeper, more intense vision, "the mystery of things," is never reached.

If (as I believe) Shakespeare is responsible for this play, his masterful hand is to be recognized only in the sureness with which he fulfilled a modest professional assignment. His aim was to celebrate the marriage of Princess Elizabeth by reminding his audience of some of the great events that preceded the birth of the first and greatest Elizabeth. He wanted to put on his stage the "very persons" of history, and to reproduce as accurately as possible the pageantry of Katherine's trial, Anne's coronation, Elizabeth's christening, which must have moved the English of that time just as the wonderful pageantry of Churchill's funeral procession moves them now. Out of these ingredients he made a show which still holds us in the theatre and makes us forget all problems of psychology or ethics, at least until we think it over.

F.F.

SUGGESTIONS FOR FURTHER READING

Further critical comments on this play will be found in Johnson, Van Doren and Webster (listed on pages 114 and 115).

Narrative and Dramatic Sources of Shakespeare, Vol. IV: Later English History Plays. Edited by Geoffrey Bullough. London and New York: 1962

This volume contains selections from Holinshed and from Foxe, Shakespeare's main sources, and from an earlier play he probably used, *When You See Me, You Know Me.* The editor contributes a very useful introduction on the problem of authorship and on the use Shakespeare made of his sources.

Knight G. Wilson. *The Crown of Life. Essays in Interpretation of Shakespeare's Final Plays.* London: 1948. (Available in paperback.)

This book contains a long essay, "Henry VIII and the Poetry of Conversion," in which the author argues that the main theme of the play is conversion to a Christian view, and that the play as a whole marks the summit of Shakespeare's life work. I cannot accept this thesis, but the essay is important, being the most careful reading of the play to appear in recent years.

A NOTE ON THE TEXT

The text of *Henry VIII* rests upon the sole authority of the Folio of 1623, in which it was first printed. The Folio text is good and clean, and offers little difficulty to the editor. The nature of the text is doubtful. Some of the stage direc-

by the General Editor 15

tions suggest literary description by the author rather than prompt-book directions. On the whole, it may seem probable that we have author's copy as its source, and there is no need to assume that double authorship compelled scribal intervention and a fair copy.

Among doubtful or disputed readings, the following have been introduced or adopted: I, i, 65, heaven gives for him; I, i, 80, fetch him in he papers; I, i, 221, Nicholas; I, ii, 67, baseness; I, ii, 139–40, This . . . point, Not . . . wish to . . . person.; I, ii, 147, Nicholas Henton; I, ii, 164, confession's seal; I, ii, 170, to win the love; I, ii, 190, Bulmer; I, iii, 39, *oui* away; II, iv, 174, A marriage; II, iv, 182, The bosom; II, iv, 183, spitting; III, i, 21, coming, now I think on't.; III, ii, 171, filled; III, ii, 343, Chattels; III, ii, 350–1, So farewell—to the little good you bear me. Farewell? A long farewell to all my greatness.; III, ii, 399, wept on him; IV, ii, 98, an earthy cold; V, iii, 11–12, frail and capable Of our flesh; V, iii, 124–6, in my presence They are too thin and base to hide offences. To me you cannot reach you play the spaniel.; V, iii, 102, 107, *Speaker's name*. Lord Chamberlain.; V, iii, 133, his place.

King Henry the Eighth: A Critical Approach

BY CHARLES J. SISSON

The historical evidence that Shakespeare wrote *King Henry the Eighth* might well seem to be beyond challenge. It is included in the First Folio edition of his plays, on the authority of his fellow actors Heminge and Condell. This is borne out by an exceptional stage memory reported in 1706 linking up its first actors with their successors at the Restoration and with its known author. Betterton in the part of King Henry, as Downes records,[1] was "instructed in it by Sir William Davenaut who had it from old Mr. Lowin, that had his instructions from Mr. Shakespeare himself." Yet comment upon the play has for long been absorbed in the discussion of Fletcher's authorship of most of it. This pattern of certainty overrides the normal perceptions of varying levels of excellence in a Shakespeare play that we find in pre-1850 criticism of *Henry the Eighth* and in the criticism of all of Shakespeare's other plays.

"The genius of Shakespeare comes in and goes out with Catherine," wrote Dr. Johnson in his notes upon the play, in "scenes which may be justly numbered among the greatest efforts of tragedy." It is disconcerting to realize that orthodox Shakespearian criticism has long maintained that the writer Shakespeare comes in and goes out with Katherine only during Acts I and II, but Fletcher during Acts III and IV. Shakespeare is also deprived of other acknowledged peaks of the play: Wolsey's famous farewell speech and his speech to Cromwell on ambition, and Cranmer's magnificent panegyric upon Elizabeth. Shakespeare is left indeed with a

[1] In *Roscius Anglicanus*, 1706, p. 25. John Lowin, one of Shakespeare's fellow actors, lived to a great age.

very modest contribution. Yet it is difficult to deny that the character whom we might call Katherine Shakespeare is one with Katherine Fletcher at all points. It will not do to contrast the mode of speech of a queen in council or in a Court trial with that of a queen among her women, and to allege differences as proof of different authorship. It is merely proof that a competent dramatist varies her mode of speech according to the circumstances of the scene, in the realism of dramatic creation.

It is significant again that much of the play derives directly from its sources in chronicles, in Holinshed and in Foxe's *Actes and Monuments,* to the extent of widespread versifying of source material. We may well boggle at the application of critical analysis that purports to identify Fletcher's exercises in paraphrase from those of Shakespeare, where both are so deeply affected by the style of Holinshed or of Foxe. In general, the intuitive perception of disparity of style, which was the original basis of Spedding's thunderbolt of 1850, lies wide open to question, and cannot claim such certainty in its application as ventures to divide Act III, Scene ii precisely at line 204. With the concept of disparity of style goes the allied concept of the essential disunity of the design of the play and its characterization, as an integral part of the orthodox theory of joint authorship. This, too, requires more critical attention than it generally receives. There are happily signs of cracks in the critical ice cap in which for so long this admirable play has been embedded.[2]

No other play of Shakespeare has been thus withdrawn from the normal approach of literary criticism, which considers a work of art as a whole. Critics of the play, for over

---

[2] *Cf.* P. Alexander, "Conjectural History, or Shakespeare's *Henry VIII,*" in *Essays and Studies,* 1951, and *King Henry VIII,* ed. R. A. Foakes. *The Arden Shakespeare,* 1957. Hazelton Spencer, in *The Art and Life of William Shakespeare,* 1940, has a revealing note. "There remains the very remote possibility that Shakespeare wrote the whole thing." . . . There are many lines which might be either Shakespeare's or Fletcher's. Neither poet is quite himself in this play."

18   *King Henry the Eighth: A Critical Approach*

a hundred years, have based their comment upon a presumed double authorship, and contentedly arrive at conclusions in harmony with a theory that, since 1850, has defined precisely the share of each author. The division then set up has been accepted as an infallible guide to most later critics and editors and has conditioned their judgments of the play. Yet at the very beginning of this criticism a whole act, Act IV, was allotted to Shakespeare, and a few months later withdrawn from him and awarded to Fletcher. Thereupon the pattern of authorship solidified into a dogma in the following form:

	SHAKESPEARE	FLETCHER
Act I	Sc. i, ii	Sc. iii, iv
Act II	Sc. iii, iv	Sc. i, ii
Act III	Sc. ii, ll. 1–203	Sc. i, Sc. ii, ll. 204–459
Act IV	———	Sc. i, ii
Act V	Sc. i	Sc. ii, iii, iv, v

The method used to arrive at this scheme forbids any hesitations concerning Act IV or any other part of this play, such as characterize even the most confident division of *The Two Noble Kinsmen* between the two writers, though E. K. Chambers allows that *"Henry VIII* is not very characteristic Fletcher."[3]

There are even signs of some uneasiness in recent years among convinced "Fletcherians." In an able survey of the question, M. Mincoff[4] finds Shakespearian quality in the imagery, the philosophy, and the dramatic power of Wolsey's great scene, Act III, Scene ii. But "the style is unquestionably" Fletcher's, he holds, who wrote the scene with the help of "suggestions" from Shakespeare. Most critics escape from similar doubts by conjecturing revision of a "Shake-

---

[3] *William Shakespeare*, I, 497. It is not, he adds, very characteristic Shakespeare either.

[4] "*Henry VIII* and Fletcher," in *Shakespeare Quarterly*, XII:3 (1961).

speare" scene by Fletcher, or a "Fletcher" scene by Shakespeare. Professor Cyrus Hoy limits Fletcher's unaided contributions to Act I, Scenes iii and iv, Act III, Scene i, Act V, Scene ii-iv, but traces his hand only as reviser or interpolator of additions to scenes by Shakespeare in Act II, Scenes i and ii, Act III, Scene ii, ll. 205ff., and Act IV, Scenes i and ii, scenes generally ascribed to Fletcher.[5] He thus preserves for Shakespeare Wolsey's great speeches in Act III, Scene ii. Such views bring us near to release from the spell of submission to the authority of an otherwise unknown critic, Hickson. It is well to turn from these partings of the garment, scene by scene, to consideration of the play as a whole.

The significance and structure of the play are closely related to the occasion of its writing and its production. Certainly this play offers a logical appendix to the series of history plays in which Shakespeare presented the Wars of the Roses and the conflict of the Houses of York and Lancaster, ending in the union of the Houses in the person of the Tudor Henry the Seventh.[6] But many years divided the writing of *Henry the Sixth* and *Richard the Third* from *Henry the Eighth*, and the fashion for history plays was long past. We cannot believe that Shakespeare, moved by artistic ambitions, formed so belated a wish to round off his history cycle, and some more immediate and direct purpose appears to be more probable.

The person of Henry the Eighth was a theme forbidden to the stage and drama during the reign of Queen Elizabeth. She would not have tolerated the presentation of her father as a stage figure, and her Lord Chamberlain, through the Master of the Revels as licensing authority, would have given short shrift to any such play, not least by his own company of actors, of which Shakespeare was a member. Two extant biographical plays sought to profit from the natural interest

---

[5] "The Shares of Fletcher and His Collaborators in The Beaumont and Fletcher Canon," in *Studies in Bibliography*, XV (1962), pp. 76ff.

[6] This has been absurdly alleged as the reason that Heminge and Condell included the play in the First Folio.

of the Elizabethans in the outstanding persons of Henry's reign. In *The Life and Death of Thomas, Lord Cromwell*, printed in 1602 and already attributed to Shakespeare, and in *The Play of Sir Thomas More*, which never reached the stage or print before modern days, the king himself makes no appearance in the *dramatis personae*. The story of Katherine's divorce and of Henry's marriage to Anne Boleyn, Elizabeth's mother, involving Elizabeth's questioned legitimacy, was plainly impossible as matter for the stage. With the accession of James the First in 1603, the subject might be said to have been "released." A new dynasty had succeeded to the throne. In 1605 Samuel Rowley's play on the reign of Henry, *When You See Me, You Know Me*, was printed as acted by Prince Henry's Men, and the king himself as well as Prince Edward, are characters in it, with a very homespun conception of Henry's unofficial activities. Katherine of Aragon and Anne Boleyn do not appear and Wolsey is a figure of wax. It bears all the signs of hasty writing for the new market. But the King's Men, and Shakespeare, still left the subject untouched.

It was not until 1613 that they produced their play, *The Famous History of the Life of King Henry the Eighth*. The evidence for its date lies in reports of the burning of the Globe Theatre during a performance of the play on 29 June 1613. It is generally assumed that these reports decide the earliest date for the play, as recording a first performance. There is good reason, however, to set its completion and first performance back to February 1613. The importance of this earlier date lies in the relation of the play to the program of dramatic entertainments arranged for the visit of the Elector Palatine and the celebration of his marriage to Princess Elizabeth. It can hardly be doubted that Shakespeare and his company designed their play with a view to the occasion for which it was intended.

As a chronicle of the life of Henry the Eighth, it responded to the general view of the outstanding feature of his reign. Elizabethan witnesses in courts of law often date events not by the year in which they occurred but in relation to notable historical happenings. For Henry's reign, such "headline" news thus recalled include the Field of the Cloth of Gold, the visit of the Emperor to England, the execution of the Duke of Buckingham, the fall of Wolsey, and the coronation of Anne Boleyn, as I find in various Chancery depositions.[7] The play covered the field of these "headlines" of the reign, and this alone was no small feat of dramatic planning. The conclusion of the play upon the birth and baptism of the baby Elizabeth seemed fitting enough to an England that for over forty years had lived under the stable rule of a queen who was heir to Henry, to his throne, to the strength and peace of his reign, and to his Reformed Church. This was his legacy to England and the fulfilment of his life. We are dealing with something more than the chronicle play of a mere sequence of events, or Rowley's makeshift hodgepodge.

No play of Shakespeare's, indeed, illustrates more fully the careful workmanship that controlled his use of his sources for dramatic ends. In his use of Holinshed and of Foxe alike, he does not restrict himself to material directly related by them to the events chronicled. As in *Macbeth,* so here he transfers elements from other contexts to heighten his dramatic effects. Wolsey's inventory of his own possessions, the immediate cause of his downfall in the play, is an element derived from Holinshed's story of the accident that befell a bishop of Durham, Thomas Ruthall, in 1508. The Chancellor's accusation of Cranmer (V, ii, ll. 42 ff.) is quoted almost verbatim from a speech of the Bishop of London to his clergy, reported by Foxe, upon another matter. So also with the historical order of events by which, in the play, Henry marries Anne Boleyn before the fall of Wolsey instead of three years after. Queen Katherine, who died in 1536, dies in the play before the birth of Elizabeth, in 1533. The effect of such deliberate changes is to create an action of continuous dramatic logic and unity.

No reader of the play and no spectator of an intelligent stage presentation of the play can escape the sense of a

---

[7] The contemporary audience would appreciate to the full the alternative title of the play reported by Wotton, *All Is True.*

22   King Henry the Eighth: A Critical Approach

deeper tragic unity that pervades this sequence of events, of an atmosphere in which its persons move. *Henry the Eighth* was a striking return to a thought that runs through the texture of *King Lear*. There the old king, denuded of power, a mere observer now of the world of statecraft, spoke to his Cordelia of court news, of "who loses, and who wins, who's in, who's out," of "packs and sects of great ones that ebb and flow by the moon." The vanity and insecurity of great place and of the ambition that pursues it color this picture of a historical reign still near to men's memories, as it had colored Shakespeare's great tragedy of ancient Britain. It is a tragic spectacle and receives tragic treatment in *Henry the Eighth*. Justice is done to Katherine, and no less to Buckingham and to Wolsey in the completeness of their portraiture and in comment upon their falls. These are not the falls of villainy at the hands of retributive justice to the full satisfaction of the beholder.[8] There is a tragic reconciliation in their fates, in which they themselves share, not merely in their acceptance of the power that rules them, but in the consequent development of their spiritual being in adversity, in which they find themselves more fully. This is especially marked in Wolsey, in a portrait that is far removed from the intolerant philippic on his life and character found by Shakespeare in Foxe. In the play, it is Wolsey himself who realizes the new-found fortitude that adversity has taught him and who charges Cromwell to fling away ambition, the evil genius by which he himself has been led.

It has not been sufficiently realized, again, how close a parallel we have in Katherine to the situation and character of Hermione in *The Winter's Tale*. There, too, we have a trial of a queen, the dice loaded heavily against her, and the final appeal from human justice to a higher power, to Apollo, as Katherine appeals to the Pope. The beauty of Shakespeare's picture of Hermione, and of the moving scene

---

[8] *Cf.* Katherine's farewell to Wolsey (IV, ii, ll. 69 ff.) and Wolsey's generous tribute to his supplanter More (III, ii, ll. 393 ff.,) both in the "Fletcher" scenes. The Epilogue singles out Katherine as an example of "good women."

of her resurrection from presumed death, should not blind us to the more complex fullness of his portrait of Katherine. There is an evident design here far beyond any mere static figure of a wronged queen. She is a living person who develops with the action of the play. True to herself in the strength of her moral being and of her royalty, she is never more herself than in her assessment, clear-sighted yet free from rancor, of her fallen enemy Wolsey, or in the blessed virtues of humility and patience that come to comfort her in adversity.

Unity of conception governs also the portrait of the king in relation to these events and persons, though critical comment has neglected the study of Shakespeare's Henry in favor of his Wolsey and Katherine, the star parts of the play. In its first half, we see Henry moving on the surface of kingship, a lover of gaiety and display, but freeing himself from the powerful persons and influences that stand near to his throne and loom too large in his realm. There is Buckingham, of royal descent, whose father helped Henry's father to the throne and who was widely loved and honored. There is Wolsey, the *novus homo,* risen through the Church, whose power he exercised to cast his immense shadow as archbishop, cardinal, and Lord Chancellor over Henry's England, and to engulf Buckingham. In the second half, Henry has broken these powers which shared his throne, these favored servants whose favor did not ensure selfless service to their master, and rules alone. So also the doing of justice moves from the course of delegated instruments to the intervention of the king, the Fountain of Justice, in his prerogative absoluteness. The pattern of his kingship has changed to that which sees him as God's deputy in England, a view that commended itself to King James. Cranmer is the servant whom he himself has created, the instrument of his policy, who owes all to him and whom he defends against his most potent enemies among the nobility or in the Church. There is no questioning of Henry's power or of his justice, even among the victims of his absoluteness, and Buckingham and Wolsey alike are submissive to the author of their fate. A striking feature of the play is the wealth of comment, a kind of linking chorus, upon its events and upon the king, in interlocutory scenes, from Sandys and the Gentlemen, so generally dismissed as irrelevancies to the action. They are integral to Shakespeare's exposition of the reign of Henry. There is every reason to relate this portrait of Henry and his kingship to the portrait of Prospero, ruler of his island in *The Tempest,* absolute in power, wise and foreseeing, implacable to evil, yet no tyrant, and deeply concerned with the hopes of the generation to come in whom reconciliation is born. The play thus falls into the pattern of Shakespeare's latest plays, with conflict resolved in a future of peace and hope, not in the triumph of Henry, but in the promise of the infant Elizabeth.

Cranmer's panegyric of Elizabeth at the end of the play foretells the succession of King James to the peaceful greatness of her reign. The marriage of James's daughter Elizabeth, the admiration of England, set the poets ablaze with images of the rebirth in her of the phoenix Queen Elizabeth, the bird of wonder in Cranmer's great speech. It was to this climax that the whole series of events in the play was directed in logical sequence, through the destruction of rival powers in England and in Rome, the king's divorce and remarriage, and the establishment of his supremacy in Church and State alike. To dismiss such a planned sequence of dramatic events as formless, desultory patchwork only explicable as the cobbling of a play by two dramatists working in an undefined scheme of collaboration, requires more evidence than that of intuition or of metrical or "linguistic" statistics. In particular, it ignores the occasion and the evident intentions of the dramatist and his company. The play, in subject and content, was admirably designed for the State occasion in question. It was lavishly produced, rich in all the developing resources of the stage and drama, in costume, masque and spectacle as in splendor of rhetoric. And a compelling inner unity of design bound together its sequence of events. The style of its writing and the pattern of its verse were inevitably affected by the material of the dramatist's plot and its projection in dramatic form, not least in the extensive inclusion of masquelike elements. Those who reject

Shakespeare's authorship of such scenes in *Henry VIII* reject also masque elements in other plays on grounds of style.[9] It is uncritical not to realize that Shakespeare was not only a genius but also a skilled professional craftsman who could adapt his writing to his purpose and his material. The spectacular use of all stage resources, and also the chorus-like comment and exposition of the Gentlemen, are features common to *Henry the Eighth* and to Shakespeare's other last plays, *Cymbeline, The Winter's Tale,* and *The Tempest.*

Shakespeare's play of *King Henry the Eighth* stands in great need of critical rehabilitation, a difficult achievement against the weight of over a hundred years of destructive comment. Some of the causes of this general disapprobation are patent. The design of the play, with its strong infusion of pageantry into a subject of historical significance, characteristic as this was not only of its occasion and purpose but of Shakespeare's latest dramatic manner, offended literary gentlemen who sought in vain for a model of epic or tragic conception comparable with those of Shakespeare's accepted masterpieces of history or of tragedy. Preconceived ideas of the proper subject of the play have beset it since the days of Pepys, who in 1664 was disappointed by Betterton as Henry, because the play did not present "the story of Henry the Eighth with all his wives," as he had been led to expect. Pepys would no doubt have welcomed the modern film production of Charles Laughton in *The Private Life of Henry the Eighth,* which shared with the variety stage his impersonation of a caricatured Holbein Henry in his later years, and gave pride of place to his matrimonial fortunes and misfortunes. Other, less elementary preferences have been put forward as designs more probable or more suitable for a play by Shakespeare on the reign of Henry the Eighth, with the elimination of the despised masques, visions, and processions strangely thought to be more characteristic of Fletcher. Plans put forward by Spedding for the rewriting

[9] E. K. Chambers, among others, treats as interpolations the ghost scene in *Richard III,* the Hymen scene in *As You Like It,* the masque in *Cymbeline,* the masque and the songs of Juno and Ceres in *The Tempest.*

of the play include a Henry punished for his disloyalty to a good Katherine, or a Katherine upstaged to allow for an Anne and Henry as heroes of the Protestant Reformation. E. K. Chambers would rewrite the part of Katherine as that of a shrew to justify Henry's desertion of her for Anne and so to remove a shadow from his reputation and an obstacle to dramatic sympathy.[10] Fletcher perhaps might have approved of such plans, but not Shakespeare.

The stars in their stage courses have also fought against Shakespeare's play. None of his plays has suffered so deeply from the surgical horrors of gross theatricalism. It is significant indeed that in 1855, some years after Spedding's and Hickson's rejection of Shakespeare, Charles Kean could boast that in his production of the play he had restored Act V, for long totally omitted. The critics, in fact, had never seen Shakespeare's play on the stage, except in grossly truncated form in which spectacle usurped still more tyrannously the action and dialogue. Kean had a conscience about the text lacking in Betterton, Garrick, Kemble and Macready. But he also bid high for pictorial effects, with a barge on the river for Buckingham, a panorama of Tudor London, and processions to rival even Garrick's coronation procession of 140 persons in 1762. In such performances, the production provided a setting for a dialogue limited to the occasions it offered for displays of rhetorical fireworks by its star performers, as in later days in Irving's famous production of 1892. The standard critical assessment of the play, in fact, reflects closely the approach of the commercial stage to its performance, and it is impossible to doubt that here the stage has influenced the study. It is something more than a coincidence that the first measured and balanced production of the play in modern times has approximated in time to the first clear steps toward a fresh critical appreciation of its qualities and its problems on the basis of

---

[10] *Shakespeare: A Survey*, p. 319.

its fully Shakespearian authorship.[11] In Tyrone Guthrie's Stratford production of 1949, under the direction of Anthony Quayle, who played Henry as England knew him, the play was Shakespeare's play, in which pageantry and drama were interfused, each heightening the impact of the other, in a continuous and rapid action leading to its climax in the promise of the succession of Elizabeth to the Tudor Henry and to his assured throne.[12]

There is, finally, no reason to doubt the authenticity of the Prologue and the Epilogue. The Prologue in particular bears close parallels to those of *Henry the Fourth Part 2,* and *Henry the Fifth,* and is a serious introduction to the play as designed and intended, including its elements of "show" to be seen among its affairs of state and the tragic spectacle of the fall of greatness.

We may reasonably feel that Shakespeare himself was in no way ashamed of his performance in this much maligned play.

---

[11] *Cf.* P. Alexander, *Shakespeare's Life and Art,* 1938; *A Shakespeare Primer,* 1951. G. W. Knight, *The Crown of Life,* 1947. H. Craig, *An Interpretation of Shakespeare,* 1948. (E. M. W. Tillyard omitted *Henry the Eighth* as of doubtful authorship from his *Shakespeare's History Plays,* 1944.)

[12] For a full account of this production, see M. St. Clare Byrne, "A Stratford Production: *Henry VIII,*" in *Shakespeare Survey,* 1950, pp. 120–29.

King Henry the Eighth

DRAMATIS PERSONAE

KING HENRY THE EIGHTH.
CARDINAL WOLSEY.
CARDINAL CAMPEIUS.
CAPUCHIUS, *ambassador from the Emperor Charles V.*
THOMAS CRANMER, *Archbishop of Canterbury.*
DUKE OF NORFOLK.
DUKE OF BUCKINGHAM.
DUKE OF SUFFOLK.
EARL OF SURREY.
LORD CHAMBERLAIN.
LORD CHANCELLOR.
STEPHEN GARDINER, *Bishop of Winchester.*
BISHOP OF LINCOLN.
LORD ABERGAVENNY.
LORD SANDYS.
SIR HENRY GUILFORD.
SIR THOMAS LOVELL.
SIR ANTHONY DENNY.
SIR NICHOLAS VAUX.
SECRETARIES *to Wolsey.*
THOMAS CROMWELL, *servant to Wolsey.*
GRIFFITH, *gentleman-usher to Queen Katherine.*
THREE GENTLEMEN.
DOCTOR BUTTS, *Physician to the King.*
GARTER KING-AT-ARMS.
SURVEYOR *to the Duke of Buckingham.*
BRANDON, *and a* SERGEANT-AT-ARMS.
DOORKEEPER *of the Council chamber.* PORTER, *and his* MAN.
PAGE *to Gardiner.* A CRIER.

KATHERINE, *Queen to King Henry, afterwards divorced.*
ANNE BULLEN, *her Maid of Honour, afterwards Queen.*
AN OLD LADY, } *attending upon Queen*
PATIENCE, } *Katherine.*

Several BISHOPS, LORDS, *and* LADIES *in the Dumb-shows;*
  WOMEN *attending upon the Queen;* CITIZENS, SCRIBES,
  OFFICERS, GUARDS, *and other* ATTENDANTS.
SPIRITS *appearing to Queen Katherine.*

SCENE—*London and Westminster; Kimbolton.*

Prologue

I come no more to make you laugh. Things now
That bear a weighty and a serious brow,
Sad, high, and working, full of state and woe,
Such noble scenes as draw the eye to flow
We now present. Those that can pity here   5
May, if they think it well, let fall a tear;
The subject will deserve it. Such as give
Their money out of hope they may believe,
May here find truth too. Those that come to see
Only a show or two, and so agree   10
The play may pass—if they be still and willing,
I'll undertake may see away their shilling
Richly in two short hours. Only they
That come to hear a merry, bawdy play,
A noise of targets, or to see a fellow   15
In a long motley coat, guarded with yellow,
Will be deceived. For gentle hearers, know,
To rank our chosen truth with such a show
As fool and fight is, beside forfeiting
Our own brains, and the opinion that we bring   20

To make that only true we now intend,
Will leave us never an understanding friend.
Therefore, for goodness' sake, and as you are
  known
The first and happiest hearers of the town,
Be sad, as we would make ye. Think ye see 25
The very persons of our noble story,
As they were living. Think you see them great,
And followed with the general throng and sweat
Of thousand friends. Then, in a moment, see
How soon this mightiness meets misery. 30
And if you can be merry then, I'll say,
A man may weep upon his wedding-day.

Act one Scene one

London. The palace.

Enter Duke of Norfolk at one door; at the other, Duke of Buckingham and Lord Abergavenny.

BUCKINGHAM
Good morrow, and well met. How have ye done
Since last we saw in France?
NORFOLK
                    I thank your Grace:
Healthful, and ever since a fresh admirer
Of what I saw there.

Act one Scene one

BUCKINGHAM
                              An untimely ague
Stayed me a prisoner in my chamber, when
Those suns of glory, those two lights of men,
Met in the vale of Andren.

NORFOLK
                              'Twixt Guines and Arde.
I was then present, saw them salute on horseback,
Beheld them when they lighted, how they clung
In their embracement, as they grew together;
Which had they, what four throned ones could have weighed
Such a compounded one?

BUCKINGHAM
                              All the whole time
I was my chamber's prisoner.

NORFOLK
                              Then you lost
The view of earthly glory. Men might say
Till this time pomp was single, but now married
To one above itself. Each following day
Became the next day's master, till the last
Made former wonders its. To-day the French,
All clinquant, all in gold, like heathen gods,
Shone down the English; and to-morrow, they
Made Britain India; every man that stood
Showed like a mine. Their dwarfish pages were
As cherubins, all gilt; the madams too,
Not used to toil, did almost sweat to bear
The pride upon them, that their very labour

Was to them as a painting. Now this masque
Was cried incomparable; and the ensuing night
Made it a fool, and beggar. The two Kings,
Equal in lustre, were now best, now worst,
As presence did present them; him in eye,
Still him in praise; and being present both,
'Twas said they saw but one, and no discerner
Durst wag his tongue in censure. When these suns—
For so they phrase 'em—by their heralds challenged
The noble spirits to arms, they did perform
Beyond thought's compass, that former fabulous story
Being now seen possible enough, got credit,
That Bevis was believed.

BUCKINGHAM
                        O you go far.

NORFOLK
As I belong to worship, and affect
In honour honesty, the tract of ev'ry thing
Would by a good discourser lose some life,
Which action's self was tongue to. All was royal,
To the disposing of it naught rebelled;
Order gave each thing view. The office did
Distinctly his full function.

BUCKINGHAM
                        Who did guide,
I mean who set the body and the limbs
Of this great sport together, as you guess?

Act one Scene one

NORFOLK
One certes, that promises no element
In such a business.

BUCKINGHAM
     I pray you who, my lord?

NORFOLK
All this was ordered by the good discretion
Of the right reverend Cardinal of York.

BUCKINGHAM
The devil speed him! No man's pie is freed
From his ambitious finger. What had he
To do in these fierce vanities? I wonder
That such a keech can with his very bulk
Take up the rays o' th' beneficial sun,
And keep it from the earth.

NORFOLK
      Surely sir,
There's in him stuff that puts him to these ends.
For being not propped by ancestry, whose grace
Chalks successors their way, nor called upon
For high feats done to th' crown, neither allied
To eminent assistants, but spider-like,
Out of his self-drawing web, 'a gives us note
The force of his own merit makes his way—
A gift that heaven gives for him, which buys
A place next to the King.

ABERGAVENNY
     I cannot tell

What heaven hath given him: let some graver eye
Pierce into that, but I can see his pride
Peep through each part of him; whence has he that?
If not from hell, the devil is a niggard,
Or has given all before, and he begins
A new hell in himself.

BUCKINGHAM
                        Why the devil,
Upon this French going out, took he upon him,
Without the privity o' th' King, to appoint
Who should attend on him? He makes up the file
Of all the gentry; for the most part such
To whom as great a charge as little honour
He meant to lay upon; and his own letter,
The honourable Board of Council out,
Must fetch him in he papers.

ABERGAVENNY
                        I do know
Kinsmen of mine, three at the least, that have
By this so sickened their estates, that never
They shall abound as formerly.

BUCKINGHAM
                        O many
Have broke their backs with laying manors on 'em
For this great journey. What did this vanity

Act one Scene one 39

But minister communication of
A most poor issue?

NORFOLK
                    Grievingly I think,
The peace between the French and us not values
The cost that did conclude it.

BUCKINGHAM
                         Every man,
After the hideous storm that followed, was
A thing inspired, and not consulting broke
Into a general prophecy—that this tempest,
Dashing the garment of this peace, aboded
The sudden breach on't.

NORFOLK
                         Which is budded out,
For France hath flawed the league, and hath
    attached
Our merchants' goods at Bordeaux.

ABERGAVENNY
                              Is it therefore
The ambassador is silenced?

NORFOLK
                         Marry is't.

ABERGAVENNY
A proper title of a peace, and purchased
At a superfluous rate.

BUCKINGHAM
                    Why all this business
Our reverend Cardinal carried.

NORFOLK

                        Like it your Grace,
The state takes notice of the private difference
Betwixt you and the Cardinal. I advise you—
And take it from a heart that wishes towards you
Honour, and plenteous safety—that you read
The Cardinal's malice and his potency
Together; to consider further, that
What his high hatred would effect wants not
A minister in his power. You know his nature,
That he's revengeful; and I know his sword
Hath a sharp edge. It's long, and't may be said,
It reaches far, and where 'twill not extend,
Thither he darts it. Bosom up my counsel,
You'll find it wholesome.

> *Enter Wolsey, the Purse borne before him; Guards, and two Secretaries with papers. Wolsey passes by Buckingham with a look of disdain, which he returns.*

                        Lo, where comes that rock
That I advise your shunning.

WOLSEY

The Duke of Buckingham's surveyor ha?
Where's his examination?

SECRETARY

                        Here so please you.

WOLSEY

Is he in person ready?

Act one Scene one

SECRETARY

                   Ay, please your Grace.

WOLSEY

Well, we shall then know more, and Buckingham
Shall lessen this big look.

        [*Exeunt Wolsey and Attendants.*

BUCKINGHAM

This butcher's cur is venom-mouthed, and I 120
Have not the power to muzzle him, therefore best
Not wake him in his slumber. A beggar's book
Outworths a noble's blood.

NORFOLK

                    What, are you chafed?
Ask God for temperance, that's the appliance only
Which your disease requires.

BUCKINGHAM

                        I read in's looks 125
Matter against me, and his eye reviled
Me as his abject object; at this instant
He bores me with some trick. He's gone to th' King.
I'll follow, and outstare him.

NORFOLK

                    Stay my lord,
And let your reason with your choler question 130
What 'tis you go about. To climb steep hills
Requires slow pace at first. Anger is like
A full hot horse, who being allowed his way

Self-mettle tires him. Not a man in England
Can advise me like you. Be to yourself 135
As you would to your friend.

BUCKINGHAM

                    I'll to the King,
And from a mouth of honour quite cry down
This Ipswich fellow's insolence; or proclaim
There's difference in no persons.

NORFOLK

                    Be advised.
Heat not a furnace for your foe so hot 140
That it do singe yourself. We may outrun
By violent swiftness that which we run at,
And lose by over-running. Know you not,
The fire that mounts the liquor till't run o'er,
In seeming to augment it, wastes it? Be advised. 145
I say again there is no English soul
More stronger to direct you than yourself,
If with the sap of reason you would quench,
Or but allay the fire of passion.

BUCKINGHAM

                Sir,
I am thankful to you, and I'll go along 150
By your prescription. But this top-proud fellow,
Whom from the flow of gall I name not, but
From sincere motions, by intelligence,
And proofs as clear as founts in July, when
We see each grain of gravel, I do know 155
To be corrupt and treasonous.

Act one Scene one

NORFOLK
>Say not treasonous.

BUCKINGHAM
To th' King I'll say't, and make my vouch as strong
As shore of rock. Attend. This holy fox,
Or wolf, or both—for he is equal ravenous
As he is subtle, and as prone to mischief 160
As able to perform't, his mind and place
Infecting one another, yea reciprocally—
Only to show his pomp, as well in France
As here at home, suggests the King our master
To this last costly treaty, the interview, 165
That swallowed so much treasure, and like a glass
Did break i' th' wrenching.

NORFOLK
>Faith, and so it did.

BUCKINGHAM
Pray give me favour sir. This cunning Cardinal
The articles o' th' combination drew
As himself pleased, and they were ratified 170
As he cried, thus let be, to as much end
As give a crutch to th' dead. But our Count-Cardinal
Has done this, and 'tis well; for worthy Wolsey,
Who cannot err, he did it. Now this follows—
Which as I take it, is a kind of puppy 175
To th' old dam treason—Charles the Emperor,

Under pretence to see the Queen his aunt—
For 'twas indeed his colour, but he came
To whisper Wolsey—here makes visitation.
His fears were that the interview betwixt 180
England and France might through their amity
Breed him some prejudice; for from this league
Peeped harms that menaced him: privily
Deals with our Cardinal; and as I trow—
Which I do well; for I am sure the Emperor 185
Paid ere he promised, whereby his suit was granted
Ere it was asked—but when the way was made,
And paved with gold, the Emperor thus desired,
That he would please to alter the King's course,
And break the foresaid peace. Let the King know, 190
As soon he shall by me, that thus the Cardinal
Does buy and sell his honour as he pleases,
And for his own advantage.

    NORFOLK

                     I am sorry
To hear this of him, and could wish he were
Something mistaken in't.

    BUCKINGHAM

                     No, not a syllable. 195
I do pronounce him in that very shape
He shall appear in proof.

    Enter Brandon, Sergeant-at-Arms, and Guard.

Act one Scene one

BRANDON
Your office sergeant, execute it.
SERGEANT
      Sir,
My Lord the Duke of Buckingham and Earl
Of Hereford, Stafford, and Northampton, I
Arrest thee of high treason, in the name
Of our most sovereign King.
BUCKINGHAM
        Lo you my lord,
The net has fallen upon me. I shall perish
Under device and practice.
BRANDON
       I am sorry
To see you ta'en from liberty, to look on
The business present. 'Tis his Highness' pleasure
You shall to th' Tower.
BUCKINGHAM
       It will help me nothing
To plead mine innocence; for that dye is on me
Which makes my whit'st part black. The will of heaven
Be done in this and all things. I obey.
O my Lord Aberga'ny, fare you well.
BRANDON
Nay, he must bear you company. [*To Aberga-venny.*] The King
Is pleased you shall to th' Tower, till you know
How he determines further.

ABERGAVENNY
                    As the duke said,
The will of heaven be done, and the King's pleasure
By me obeyed.
    BRANDON
                    Here is a warrant from
The King t' attach Lord Montacute, and the bodies
Of the duke's confessor, John de la Car,
One Gilbert Peck, his councillor—
    BUCKINGHAM
                            So, so;
These are the limbs o' th' plot. No more, I hope.
    BRANDON
A monk o' th' Chartreux.
    BUCKINGHAM
                        O Nicholas Hopkins?
    BRANDON
                                He.
    BUCKINGHAM
My surveyor is false. The o'er-great Cardinal
Hath showed him gold; my life is spanned already.
I am the shadow of poor Buckingham,
Whose figure even this instant cloud puts on,
By darkening my clear sun. My lord, farewell.
                        [*Exeunt.*

Scene two

The same.

Flourish. Enter Henry, leaning on Wolsey; Lords of Council; Sir Thomas Lovell, Wolsey's Secretary. Henry takes his throne. Wolsey sits at his feet, on his right.

HENRY
My life itself, and the best heart of it,
Thanks you for this great care. I stood i' th' level
Of a full-charged confederacy, and give thanks
To you that choked it. Let be called before us
That gentleman of Buckingham's: in person 5
I'll hear him his confessions justify,
And point by point the treasons of his master
He shall again relate.
Voice within, Room for the Queen. *Enter Katherine, ushered by the Dukes of Norfolk and Suffolk: she kneels. Henry rises from his throne, raises her, kisses and places her by him.*

KATHERINE
Nay, we must longer kneel; I am a suitor.

HENRY

Arise, and take place by us. Half your suit
Never name to us; you have half our power.
The other moiety ere you ask is given.
Repeat your will, and take it.

KATHERINE

Thank your Majesty.
That you would love yourself, and in that love
Not unconsidered leave your honour, nor
The dignity of your office, is the point
Of my petition.

HENRY

Lady mine, proceed.

KATHERINE

I am solicited not by a few,
And those of true condition, that your subjects
Are in great grievance. There have been commissions
Sent down among 'em, which hath flawed the heart
Of all their loyalties; wherein, although
My good Lord Cardinal, they vent reproaches
Most bitterly on you, as putter on
Of these exactions, yet the King our master,
Whose honour heaven shield from soil, even he escapes not
Language unmannerly, yea, such which breaks
The sides of loyalty, and almost appears
In loud rebellion.

Act one Scene two

NORFOLK
                    Not almost appears.
It doth appear. For upon these taxations,
The clothiers all, not able to maintain
The many to them longing, have put off
The spinsters, carders, fullers, weavers, who
Unfit for other life, compelled by hunger
And lack of other means, in desperate manner
Daring th' event to th' teeth, are all in uproar,
And danger serves among them.
    HENRY
                        Taxation?
Wherein? And what taxation? My Lord
   Cardinal,
You that are blamed for it alike with us,
Know you of this taxation?
    WOLSEY
                        Please you sir,
I know but of a single part in aught
Pertains to th' state, and front but in that file
Where others tell steps with me.
    KATHERINE
                        No, my lord?
You know no more than others? But you frame
Thing that are known alike, which are not
   wholesome
To those which would not know them, and yet
   must
Perforce be their acquaintance. These exactions,
Whereof my sovereign would have note, they are

Most pestilent to th' hearing; and to bear 'em,
The back is sacrifice to th' load. They say
They are devised by you, or else you suffer
Too hard an exclamation.
  HENRY
                    Still exaction!
The nature of it? In what kind, let's know,
Is this exaction?
  KATHERINE
                    I am much too venturous
In tempting of your patience, but am boldened
Under your promised pardon. The subjects' grief
Comes through commissions, which compels from each
The sixth part of his substance, to be levied
Without delay; and the pretence for this
Is named, your wars in France. This makes bold mouths.
Tongues spit their duties out, and cold hearts freeze
Allegiance in them; their curses now
Live where their prayers did; and it's come to pass,
This tractable obedience is a slave
To each incensed will. I would your Highness
Would give it quick consideration, for
There is no primer baseness.
  HENRY
                         By my life,
This is against our pleasure.

Act one Scene two

WOLSEY
                    And for me,
I have no further gone in this than by
A single voice, and that not passed me but
By learned approbation of the judges. If I am
Traduced by ignorant tongues, which neither know
My faculties nor person, yet will be
The chronicles of my doing, let me say
'Tis but the fate of place, and the rough brake
That virtue must go through. We must not stint
Our necessary actions, in the fear
To cope malicious censurers, which ever
As ravenous fishes do a vessel follow
That is new-trimmed, but benefit no further
Than vainly longing. What we oft do best,
By sick interpreters, once weak ones, is
Not ours, or not allowed; what worst, as oft,
Hitting a grosser quality, is cried up
For our best act. If we shall stand still,
In fear our motion will be mocked, or carped at,
We should take root here where we sit,
Or sit state-statues only.

HENRY
                    Things done well,
And with a care, exempt themselves from fear.
Things done without example, in their issue
Are to be feared. Have you a precedent
Of this commission? I believe, not any.
We must not rend our subjects from our laws,

And stick them in our will. Sixth part of each?
A trembling contribution. Why, we take
From every tree lop, bark, and part o' th' timber;
And though we leave it with a root, thus hacked,
The air will drink the sap. To every county
Where this is questioned send our letters, with
Free pardon to each man that has denied
The force of this commission. Pray look to't;
I put it to your care.

WOLSEY [*to Secretary*]

A word with you.
Let there be letters writ to every shire,
Of the King's grace and pardon. [*Aside to him.*]
  The grieved commons
Hardly conceive of me. Let it be noised
That through our intercession this revokement
And pardon comes. I shall anon advise you
Further in the proceeding.   [*Exit Secretary.*

Enter Surveyor.

KATHERINE

I am sorry that the Duke of Buckingham
Is run in your displeasure.

HENRY

                It grieves many.
The gentleman is learned, and a most rare
  speaker;
To nature none more bound; his training such,
That he may furnish and instruct great teachers,
And never seek for aid out of himself. Yet see,
When these so noble benefits shall prove

Act one Scene two

Not well disposed, the mind growing once
 corrupt,
They turn to vicious forms, ten times more ugly
Than ever they were fair. This man so complete,
Who was enrolled 'mongst wonders, and when
 we
Almost with ravished listening could not find
His hour of speech a minute; he my lady,
Hath into monstrous habits put the graces
That once were his, and is become as black
As if besmeared in hell. Sit by us, you shall
 hear—
This was his gentleman in trust—of him
Things to strike honour sad. Bid him recount
The fore-recited practices, whereof
We cannot feel too little, hear too much.
WOLSEY
Stand forth, and with bold spirit relate what you
Most like a careful subject have collected
Out of the Duke of Buckingham.
HENRY
                         Speak freely.
SURVEYOR
First, it was usual with him—every day
It would infect his speech—that if the King
Should without issue die, he'll carry it so
To make the sceptre his. These very words
I've heard him utter to his son-in-law,
Lord Aberga'ny; to whom by oath he menaced
Revenge upon the Cardinal.

WOLSEY
                    Please your Highness note
This dangerous conception in this point,
Not friended by his wish to your high person.   140
His will is most malignant, and it stretches
Beyond you to your friends.

KATHERINE
                    My learned Lord Cardinal,
Deliver all with charity.

HENRY
                    Speak on.
How grounded he his title to the crown
Upon our fail? To this point hast thou heard him   145
At any time speak aught?

SURVEYOR
                    He was brought to this
By a vain prophecy of Nicholas Henton.

HENRY
What was that Henton?

SURVEYOR
                    Sir, a Chartreux friar,
His confessor, who fed him every minute
With words of sovereignty.

HENRY
                    How know'st thou this?   150

SURVEYOR
Not long before your Highness sped to France,
The duke being at the Rose, within the parish
Saint Lawrence Poultney, did of me demand
What was the speech among the Londoners,

Act one Scene two

Concerning the French journey. I replied, 155
Men feared the French would prove perfidious,
To the King's danger. Presently the duke
Said, 'twas the fear indeed, and that he doubted
'Twould prove the verity of certain words
Spoke by a holy monk, that oft, says he, 160
Hath sent to me, wishing me to permit
John de la Car, my chaplain, a choice hour
To hear from him a matter of some moment;
Whom after under the confession's seal
He solemnly had sworn, that what he spoke 165
My chaplain to no creature living but
To me should utter, with demure confidence
This pausingly ensued, neither the King nor's heirs,
Tell you the duke, shall prosper, bid him strive
To win the love o' th' commonalty; the duke 170
Shall govern England.

    KATHERINE

                If I know you well,
You were the duke's surveyor, and lost your office
On the complaint o' th' tenants. Take good heed 175
You charge not in your spleen a noble person,
And spoil your nobler soul. I say, take heed;
Yes, heartily beseech you.

    HENRY

                Let him on.
Go forward.

SURVEYOR
On my soul, I'll speak but truth.
I told my lord the duke, by th' devil's illusions
The monk might be deceived, and that 'twas dangerous
For him to ruminate on this so far, until
It forged him some design, which being believed,
It was much like to do. He answered, tush,
It can do me no damage; adding further,
That had the King in his last sickness failed,
The Cardinal's and Sir Thomas Lovell's heads
Should have gone off.

HENRY
Ha! What, so rank? Aha,
There's mischief in this man; canst thou say further?

SURVEYOR
I can my liege.

HENRY
Proceed.

SURVEYOR
Being at Greenwich,
After your Highness had reproved the duke
About Sir William Bulmer—

HENRY
I remember
Of such a time. Being my sworn servant,
The duke retained him his. But on, what hence?

SURVEYOR
If, quoth he, I for this had been committed,

Act one Scene two

As to the Tower, I thought, I would have played
The part my father meant to act upon 195
The usurper Richard, who being at Salisbury,
Made suit to come in's presence; which if granted,
As he made semblance of his duty, would
Have put his knife into him.

HENRY
                        A giant traitor.

WOLSEY
Now madam, may his Highness live in freedom, 200
And this man out of prison?

KATHERINE
                         God mend all.

HENRY
There's something more would out of thee; what sayst?

SURVEYOR
After, the duke his father, with, the knife,
He stretched him, and with one hand on his dagger
Another spread on's breast, mounting his eyes, 205
He did discharge a horrible oath, whose tenour
Was, were he evil used, he would outgo
His father, by as much as a performance
Does an irresolute purpose.

HENRY
                      There's his period,
To sheathe his knife in us. He is attached; 210

Call him to present trial. If he may
Find mercy in the law, 'tis his; if none,
Let him not seek't of us. By day and night,
He's traitor to th' height. [*Exeunt.*

Scene three

The same.

Enter Lord Chamberlain and Lord Sandys.

LORD CHAMBERLAIN
Is't possible the spells of France should juggle
Men into such strange mysteries?
SANDYS
                              New customs,
Though they be never so ridiculous,
Nay let 'em be unmanly, yet are followed.
LORD CHAMBERLAIN
As far as I see, all the good our English   5
Have got by the late voyage is but merely
A fit or two o' th' face; but they are shrewd ones;
For when they hold 'em, you would swear directly
Their very noses had been councillors
To Pepin or Clotharius, they keep state so.   10
SANDYS
They have all new legs, and lame ones; one would take it,

Act one Scene three

That never saw 'em pace before, the spavin
Or springhalt reigned among 'em.
    LORD CHAMBERLAIN
                          Death, my lord,
Their clothes are after such a pagan cut to't,
That sure th' have worn out Christendom.
Enter Lovell.
                                How now,
What news, Sir Thomas Lovell?
    LOVELL
                           Faith my lord,
I hear of none but the new proclamation,
That's clapped upon the court gate.
    LORD CHAMBERLAIN
                            What is't for?
    LOVELL
The reformation of our travelled gallants,
That fill the Court with quarrels, talk, and tailors.
    LORD CHAMBERLAIN
I'm glad 'tis there; now I would pray our monsieurs
To think an English courtier may be wise,
And never see the Louvre.
    LOVELL
                      They must either—
For so run the conditions—leave those remnants
Of fool and feather, that they got in France,
With all their honourable points of ignorance

Pertaining thereunto—as fights and fireworks,
Abusing better men than they can be
Out of a foreign wisdom—renouncing clean
The faith they have in tennis and tall stockings,
Short blistered breeches, and those types of travel,
And understand again like honest men;
Or pack to their old playfellows. There, I take it,
They may cum privilegio oui away
The lag end of their lewdness, and be laughed at.

SANDYS
'Tis time to give 'em physic, their diseases
Are grown so catching.

LORD CHAMBERLAIN
                What a loss our ladies
Will have of these trim vanities.

LOVELL
                    Ay marry,
There will be woe indeed lords, the sly whoresons
Have got a speeding trick to lay down ladies.
A French song, and a fiddle, has no fellow.

SANDYS
The devil fiddle 'em, I am glad they are going,
For sure there's no converting of 'em. Now
An honest country lord, as I am, beaten
A long time out of play, may bring his plainsong,
And have an hour of hearing, and by'r lady
Held current music too.

Act one Scene three

LORD CHAMBERLAIN
                    Well said Lord Sandys,
Your colt's tooth is not cast yet.
    SANDYS
                        No my lord,
Nor shall not while I have a stump.
    LORD CHAMBERLAIN
                            Sir Thomas,
Whither were you a-going?
    LOVELL
                    To the Cardinal's.
Your lordship is a guest too.
    LORD CHAMBERLAIN
                        O, 'tis true.
This night he makes a supper, and a great one,
To many lords and ladies; there will be
The beauty of this kingdom, I'll assure you.
    LOVELL
That churchman bears a bounteous mind indeed,
A hand as fruitful as the land that feeds us;
His dews fall every where.
    LORD CHAMBERLAIN
                        No doubt he's noble;
He had a black mouth that said other of him.
    SANDYS
He may, my lord; has wherewithal. In him
Sparing would show a worse sin than ill doctrine.
Men of his way should be most liberal,
They are set here for examples.

LORD CHAMBERLAIN
                          True, they are so;
But few now give so great ones. My barge stays;
Your lordship shall along. Come, good Sir Thomas,
We shall be late else; which I would not be,
For I was spoke to, with Sir Henry Guilford,
This night to be comptrollers.
      SANDYS
                I am your lordship's.   [*Exeunt.*

Scene four

York Place. The presence chamber.

Hautboys. A state set, with a small table, also a larger table. Enter Anne Bullen with Ladies and Gentlemen at one door; at another, Sir Henry Guilford.

      GUILFORD
Ladies, a general welcome from his Grace
Salutes ye all. This night he dedicates
To fair content, and you. None here he hopes
In all this noble bevy, has brought with her
One care abroad; he would have all as merry
As first, good company, good wine, good welcome,
Can make good people.
      Enter Lord Chamberlain, Sandys, and Lovell.
                          O my lord, y'are tardy;

Act one Scene four

The very thought of this fair company
Clapped wings to me.
>LORD CHAMBERLAIN
>>You are young, Sir Harry Guilford.
>SANDYS

Sir Thomas Lovell, had the Cardinal
But half my lay thoughts in him, some of these
Should find a running banquet ere they rested,
I think would better please 'em. By my life,
They are a sweet society of fair ones.
>LOVELL

O that your lordship were but now confessor
To one or two of these.
>SANDYS
>>I would I were;

They should find easy penance.
>LOVELL
>>>Faith, how easy?
>SANDYS

As easy as a down bed would afford it.
>LORD CHAMBERLAIN

Sweet ladies, will it please you sit? Sir Harry,
Place you that side, I'll take the charge of this.
His Grace is entering. Nay, you must not freeze.
Two women placed together makes cold weather.
My Lord Sandys, you are one will keep 'em waking;
Pray sit between these ladies.

SANDYS
                    By my faith,
And thank your lordship. By your leave sweet
    ladies.   [*Sits next to Anne.*
If I chance to talk a little wild, forgive me.
I had it from my father.
ANNE
                    Was he mad sir?
SANDYS
O very mad, exceeding mad, in love too.
But he would bite none; just as I do now,
He would kiss you twenty with a breath.
                                [*Kisses her.*
LORD CHAMBERLAIN
                    Well said my lord.
So now y'are fairly seated. Gentlemen,
The penance lies on you, if these fair ladies
Pass away frowning.
SANDYS
                For my little cure,
Let me alone.
    *Hautboys. Enter Wolsey, attended, and
    takes his state.*
WOLSEY
Y'are welcome my fair guests; that noble lady
Or gentleman that is not freely merry
Is not my friend. This to confirm my welcome,
And to you all good health.   [*Drinks.*
SANDYS
                Your Grace is noble.

Act one Scene four

Let me have such a bowl may hold my thanks,
And save me so much talking.
>   WOLSEY
>   My Lord Sandys,
> I am beholding to you: cheer your neighbours.
> Ladies you are not merry: gentlemen,
> Whose fault in this?
>   SANDYS
>   The red wine first must rise
> In their fair cheeks, my lord, then we shall have 'em
> Talk us to silence.
>   ANNE
>   You are a merry gamester
> My Lord Sandys.
>   SANDYS
>   Yes, if I make my play.
> Here's to your ladyship, and pledge it madam,
> For 'tis to such a thing—
>   ANNE
>   You cannot show me.
>   SANDYS
> I told your Grace they would talk anon.
>   [*Drum and trumpet; chambers discharged*.
>   WOLSEY
>   What's that?
>   LORD CHAMBERLAIN
> Look out there, some of ye.   [*Exit Servant*.

WOLSEY
What warlike voice,
And to what end, is this? Nay ladies, fear not;
By all the laws of war y'are privileged.
Enter Servant.
LORD CHAMBERLAIN
How now, what is't?
SERVANT
A noble troop of strangers,
For so they seem; th'have left their barge, and landed,
And hither make, as great ambassadors
From foreign princes.
WOLSEY
Good Lord Chamberlain,
Go give 'em welcome; you can speak the French tongue;
And pray receive 'em nobly, and conduct 'em
Into our presence, where this heaven of beauty
Shall shine at full upon them. Some attend him.
[*Exit Lord Chamberlain, attended. All rise, and tables removed.*
You have now a broken banquet, but we'll mend it.
A good digestion to you all, and once more
I shower a welcome on ye—welcome all.
Hautboys. Enter Henry and others, as Masquers, habited like shepherds, ushered by the Lord Chamberlain. They

Act one Scene four

> *pass directly before Wolsey, and gracefully salute him.*

A noble company. What are their pleasures?

LORD CHAMBERLAIN

Because they speak no English, thus they prayed
To tell your Grace; that having heard by fame
Of this so noble and so fair assembly,
This night to meet here, they could do no less,
Out of the great respect they bear to beauty,
But leave their flocks, and under your fair conduct,
Crave leave to view these ladies, and entreat
An hour of revels with 'em.

WOLSEY

Say, Lord Chamberlain,
They have done my poor house grace; for which I pay 'em
A thousand thanks, and pray 'em take their pleasures.

[*The Masquers choose Ladies, Henry chooses Anne.*

HENRY

The fairest hand I ever touched. O beauty,
Till now I never knew thee. [*Music. Dance.*

WOLSEY

My lord—

LORD CHAMBERLAIN
Your Grace.

WOLSEY

Pray tell 'em thus much from me:

There should be one amongst 'em, by his person,
More worthy this place than myself, to whom,
If I but knew him, with my love and duty
I would surrender it.
>LORD CHAMBERLAIN
>>I will my lord.
>>>[*Whispers the Masquers.*

>WOLSEY

What say they?
>LORD CHAMBERLAIN
>>Such a one, they all confess
There is indeed, which they would have your Grace
Find out, and he will take it.
>WOLSEY
>>Let me see then.
By all your good leaves gentlemen—here I'll make
My royal choice.
>HENRY
>>Ye have found him Cardinal.
>>>[*Unmasks.*
You hold a fair assembly; you do well lord.
You are a churchman, or I'll tell you, Cardinal,
I should judge now unhappily.
>WOLSEY
>>I am glad
Your Grace is grown so pleasant.
>HENRY
>>My Lord Chamberlain.

Act one Scene four

Prithee come hither. What fair lady's that?
>LORD CHAMBERLAIN

An't please your Grace, Sir Thomas Bullen's daughter,
The Viscount Rochford, one of her Highness' women.
>HENRY

By heaven she is a dainty one. Sweetheart,
I were unmannerly to take you out,
And not to kiss you [*kisses her*]. A health gentlemen.
Let it go round.
>WOLSEY

Sir Thomas Lovell, is the banquet ready
I' th' privy chamber?
>LOVELL

        Yes, my lord.
>WOLSEY

           Your Grace
I fear with dancing is a little heated.
>HENRY

I fear, too much.
>WOLSEY

      There's fresher air my lord,
In the next chamber.
>HENRY

Lead in your ladies every one. Sweet partner,
I must not yet forsake you. Let's be merry.
Good my Lord Cardinal, I have half a dozen healths

70　　　　　　　　　　*King Henry the Eighth*

To drink to these fair ladies, and a measure　105
To lead 'em once again; and then let's dream
Who's best in favour. Let the music knock it.
　　　　　　　[*Exeunt with trumpets.*

Act two Scene one

London. A street.

Enter two Gentlemen, at several doors, meeting.

FIRST GENTLEMAN
Whither away so fast?
SECOND GENTLEMAN
O, God save ye.
Ev'n to the hall, to hear what shall become
Of the great Duke of Buckingham.
FIRST GENTLEMAN
I'll save you
That labour sir. All's now done but the ceremony
Of bringing back the prisoner.
SECOND GENTLEMAN
Were you there?   5
FIRST GENTLEMAN
Yes indeed was I.
SECOND GENTLEMAN
Pray speak what has happened.
FIRST GENTLEMAN
You may guess quickly what.

SECOND GENTLEMAN

                          Is he found guilty?

FIRST GENTLEMAN

Yes truly is he, and condemned upon't.

SECOND GENTLEMAN

I am sorry for't.

FIRST GENTLEMAN

            So are a number more.

SECOND GENTLEMAN

But pray how passed it?

FIRST GENTLEMAN

I'll tell you in a little. The great duke
Came to the bar; where to his accusations
He pleaded still not guilty, and alleged
Many sharp reasons to defeat the law.
The King's attorney, on the contrary,
Urged on the examinations, proofs, confessions
Of divers witnesses, which the duke desired
To have brought viva voce to his face;
At which appeared against him his surveyor,
Sir Gilbert Peck his chancellor, and John Car,
Confessor to him, with that devil-monk
Hopkins, that made this mischief.

SECOND GENTLEMAN

                         That was he
That fed him with his prophecies.

FIRST GENTLEMAN

                         The same.
All these accused him strongly, which he fain

Act two Scene one

Would have flung from him, but indeed he
  could not.
And so his peers upon this evidence
Have found him guilty of high treason. Much
He spoke, and learnedly, for life. But all
Was either pitied in him, or forgotten.

SECOND GENTLEMAN
After all this, how did he bear himself?

FIRST GENTLEMAN
When he was brought again to th' bar, to hear
His knell rung out, his judgement, he was stirred
With such an agony, he sweat extremely,
And something spoke in choler, ill, and hasty.
But he fell to himself again, and sweetly
In all the rest showed a most noble patience.

SECOND GENTLEMAN
I do not think he fears death.

FIRST GENTLEMAN
                    Sure he does not,
He never was so womanish; the cause
He may a little grieve at.

SECOND GENTLEMAN
                    Certainly
The Cardinal is the end of this.

FIRST GENTLEMAN
                    'Tis likely,
By all conjectures. First Kildare's attainder,
Then deputy of Ireland; who removed,
Earl Surrey was sent thither, and in haste too,
Lest he should help his father.

SECOND GENTLEMAN
                    That trick of state
Was a deep envious one.
    FIRST GENTLEMAN
                    At his return
No doubt he will requite it. This is noted,
And generally, whoever the King favours,
The Cardinal instantly will find employment,
And far enough from Court too.
    SECOND GENTLEMAN
                    All the commons
Hate him perniciously, and o' my conscience
Wish him ten fathom deep. This duke as much
They love and dote on, call him bounteous
  Buckingham,
The mirror of all courtesy.

> *Enter Buckingham; tipstaves before him, the axe with the edge towards him; halberds on each side; Lovell, Vaux, Sandys, and Citizens.*

    FIRST GENTLEMAN
                    Stay there sir,
And see the noble ruined man you speak of.
    SECOND GENTLEMAN
Let's stand close and behold him.
    BUCKINGHAM
                    All good people,
You that thus far have come to pity me,
Hear what I say, and then go home and lose me.
I have this day received a traitor's judgement,

Act two Scene one

And by that name must die: yet heaven bear witness,
And if I have a conscience, let it sink me, 60
Even as the axe falls, if I be not faithful.
The law I bear no malice for my death,
'T has done upon the premises but justice.
But those that sought it I could wish more Christians.
Be what they will, I heartily forgive 'em. 65
Yet let 'em look they glory not in mischief,
Nor build their evils on the graves of great men;
For then my guiltless blood must cry against 'em.
For further life in this world I ne'er hope,
Nor will I sue, although the King have mercies 70
More than I dare make faults. You few that loved me,
And dare be bold to weep for Buckingham,
His noble friends and fellows, whom to leave
Is only bitter to him, only dying,
Go with me like good angels to my end, 75
And as the long divorce of steel falls on me,
Make of your prayers one sweet sacrifice,
And lift my soul to heaven. Lead on a God's name.

LOVELL

I do beseech your Grace, for charity,
If ever any malice in your heart 80
Were hid against me, now to forgive me frankly.

BUCKINGHAM

Sir Thomas Lovell, I as free forgive you

As I would be forgiven. I forgive all.
There cannot be those numberless offences
'Gainst me, that I cannot take peace with. No black envy
Shall mark my grave. Commend me to his Grace;
And if he speak of Buckingham, pray tell him,
You met him half in heaven. My vows and prayers
Yet are the King's; and till my soul forsake,
Shall cry for blessings on him. May he live
Longer than I have time to tell his years.
Ever beloved and loving may his rule be.
And when old time shall lead him to his end,
Goodness and he fill up one monument.
　　　LOVELL
To the water-side I must conduct your Grace,
Then give my charge up to Sir Nicholas Vaux,
Who undertakes you to your end.
　　　VAUX
　　　　　　　　　　Prepare there,
The duke is coming. See the barge be ready,
And fit it with such furniture as suits
The greatness of his person.
　　　BUCKINGHAM
　　　　　　　　　　Nay, Sir Nicholas,
Let it alone, my state now will but mock me.
When I came hither, I was Lord High Constable
And Duke of Buckingham; now, poor Edward Bohun.

Act two Scene one

Yet I am richer than my base accusers,
That never knew what truth meant. I now seal it; 105
And with that blood will make 'em one day groan for't.
My noble father, Henry of Buckingham,
Who first raised head against usurping Richard,
Flying for succour to his servant Banister,
Being distressed, was by that wretch betrayed, 110
And without trial fell; God's peace be with him.
Henry the Seventh succeeding, truly pitying
My father's loss, like a most royal Prince,
Restored me to my honours, and out of ruins
Made my name once more noble. Now his son, 115
Henry the Eight, life, honour, name, and all
That made me happy, at one stroke has taken
For ever from the world. I had my trial,
And must needs say a noble one; which makes me
A little happier than my wretched father. 120
Yet thus far we are one in fortunes; both
Fell by our servants, by those men we loved most.
A most unnatural and faithless service.
Heaven has an end in all: yet, you that hear me,
This from a dying man receive as certain: 125
Where you are liberal of your loves and counsels,
Be sure you be not loose; for those you make friends,

And give your hearts to, when they once perceive
The least rub in your fortunes, fall away
Like water from ye, never found again   130
But where they mean to sink ye. All good people,
Pray for me. I must now forsake ye. The last hour
Of my long weary life is come upon me.
Farewell; and when you would say something that is sad,   135
Speak how I fell. I have done; and God forgive me.   [*Exeunt Buckingham and Attendants.*

    FIRST GENTLEMAN
O, this is full of pity. Sir, it calls,
I fear, too many curses on their heads
That were the authors.

    SECOND GENTLEMAN
              If the duke be guiltless,
'Tis full of woe; yet I can give you inkling   140
Of an ensuing evil, if it fall,
Greater than this.

    FIRST GENTLEMAN
              Good angels keep it from us.
What may it be? You do not doubt my faith sir?

    SECOND GENTLEMAN
This secret is so weighty, 'twill require
A strong faith to conceal it.

    FIRST GENTLEMAN
              Let me have it.   145
I do not talk much.

Act two Scene one 79

SECOND GENTLEMAN
                I am confident;
You shall sir. Did you not of late days hear
A buzzing of a separation
Between the King and Katherine?
    FIRST GENTLEMAN
                            Yes, but it held not;
For when the King once heard it, out of anger   150
He sent command to the Lord Mayor straight
To stop the rumour, and allay those tongues
That durst disperse it.
    SECOND GENTLEMAN
                       But that slander sir,
Is found a truth now, for it grows again
Fresher than e'er it was, and held for certain   155
The King will venture at it. Either the Cardinal,
Or some about him near, have out of malice
To the good Queen, possessed him with a scruple
That will undo her. To confirm this too,
Cardinal Campeius is arrived, and lately;   160
As all think, for this business.
    FIRST GENTLEMAN
                          'Tis the Cardinal;
And merely to revenge him on the Emperor,
For not bestowing on him at his asking
The archbishopric of Toledo, this is purposed.
    SECOND GENTLEMAN
I think you have hit the mark; but is't not cruel   165
That she should feel the smart of this? The
  Cardinal

80   King Henry the Eighth

Will have his will, and she must fall.
>FIRST GENTLEMAN

                                    'Tis woful.
We are too open here to argue this.
Let's think in private more.   [*Exeunt.*

Scene two

> *London. The palace.*
>
> *Enter Lord Chamberlain, reading a letter.*

LORD CHAMBERLAIN

My Lord, the horses your Lordship sent for, with all the care I had, I saw well chosen, ridden, and furnished. They were young and handsome, and of the best breed in the North. When they were ready to set out for London, a man of my Lord Cardinal's, by commission and main power, took 'em from me, with this reason: his master would be served before a subject, if not before the King, which stopped our mouths sir.

I fear he will indeed; well, let him have them;
He will have all I think.

> *Enter Norfolk and Suffolk.*

NORFOLK

Well met my Lord Chamberlain.

LORD CHAMBERLAIN

Good day to both your Graces.

SUFFOLK

How is the King employed?

Act two Scene two   81
>LORD CHAMBERLAIN
                              I left him private,   15
Full of sad thoughts and troubles.
>NORFOLK
                                   What's the cause?
>LORD CHAMBERLAIN
It seems the marriage with his brother's wife
Has crept too near his conscience.
>SUFFOLK
                              No, his conscience
Has crept too near another lady.
>NORFOLK
                                        'Tis so.
This is the Cardinal's doing, the King-Cardinal.   20
That blind priest, like the eldest son of fortune,
Turns what he list. The King will know him one day.
>SUFFOLK
Pray God he do, he'll never know himself else.
>NORFOLK
How holily he works in all his business,
And with what zeal! For now he has cracked the league   25
Between us and the Emperor, the Queen's great nephew,
He dives into the King's soul, and there scatters
Dangers, doubts, wringing of the conscience,
Fears, and despairs, and all these for his marriage.
And out of all these, to restore the King,   30
He counsels a divorce, a loss of her

That like a jewel has hung twenty years
About his neck, yet never lost her lustre;
Of her that loves him with that excellence
That angels love good men with; even of her 35
That when the greatest stroke of fortune falls
Will bless the King. And is not this course pious?
    LORD CHAMBERLAIN
Heaven keep me from such counsel. 'Tis most true
These news are everywhere, every tongue speaks 'em,
And every true heart weeps for't. All that dare 40
Look into these affairs see this main end,
The French King's sister. Heaven will one day open
The King's eyes, that so long have slept upon
This bold bad man.
    SUFFOLK
                And free us from his slavery.
    NORFOLK
We had need pray, 45
And heartily, for our deliverance;
Or this imperious man will work us all
From princes into pages: all men's honours
Lie like one lump before him, to be fashioned
Into what pitch he please.
    SUFFOLK
                For me, my lords, 50
I love him not, nor fear him, there's my creed.
As I am made without him, so I'll stand,

Act two Scene two

If the King please. His curses and his blessings
Touch me alike; th'are breath I not believe in.
I knew him, and I know him; so I leave him
To him that made him proud, the Pope.

NORFOLK

                            Let's in:
And with some other business put the King
From these sad thoughts, that work too much upon him.
My lord, you'll bear us company?

LORD CHAMBERLAIN

                            Excuse me;
The King has sent me otherwhere. Besides,
You'll find a most unfit time to disturb him:
Health to your lordships.

NORFOLK

    Thanks my good Lord Chamberlain.

[*Exit Lord Chamberlain. Henry draws the curtain, discovering himself. He sits down, and reads.*

SUFFOLK

How sad he looks, sure he is much afflicted.

HENRY

Who's there, ha?

NORFOLK

        Pray God he be not angry.

HENRY

Who's there I say. How dare you thrust yourselves
Into my private meditations?

Who am I, ha?

NORFOLK

A gracious King that pardons all offences
Malice ne'er meant. Our breach of duty this way
Is business of estate, in which we come
To know your royal pleasure.

HENRY

                    Ye are too bold.
Go to, I'll make ye know your times of business.
Is this an hour for temporal affairs? Ha?

Enter Wolsey and Campeius, with a Commission.

Who's there? My good Lord Cardinal? O my Wolsey,
The quiet of my wounded conscience;
Thou art a cure fit for a King. [*To Campeius.*] You're welcome,
Most learned reverend sir, into our kingdom:
Use us, and it. [*To Wolsey.*] My good lord, have great care
I be not found a talker.

WOLSEY

                Sir, you cannot.
I would your Grace would give us but an hour
Of private conference.

HENRY [*to Norfolk and Suffolk*]

                We are busy; go.

NORFOLK [*aside to Suffolk*]

This priest has no pride in him?

Act two Scene two   85

SUFFOLK [*aside to Norfolk*]
                    Not to speak of.
I would not be so sick though for his place.
But this cannot continue.
    NORFOLK [*aside to Suffolk*]
                    If it do,
I'll venture one have at him.
    SUFFOLK [*aside to Norfolk*]
                    I another.   85
        [*Exeunt Norfolk and Suffolk.*
    WOLSEY
Your Grace has given a precedent of wisdom
Above all princes, in committing freely
Your scruple to the voice of Christendom.
Who can be angry now? What envy reach you?
The Spaniard, tied by blood and favour to her,   90
Must now confess, if they have any goodness,
The trial just and noble. All the clerks,
I mean the learned ones, in Christian kingdoms,
Have their free voices; Rome, the nurse of
  judgement,
Invited by your noble self, hath sent   95
One general tongue unto us, this good man,
This just and learned priest, Cardinal Campeius,
Whom once more I present unto your Highness.
    HENRY
And once more in mine arms I bid him welcome,
And thank the holy conclave for their loves.   100
They have sent me such a man I would have
  wished for.

CAMPEIUS

Your Grace must needs deserve all strangers' loves,
You are so noble. To your Highness' hand
I tender my commission; by whose virtue,
The Court of Rome commanding, you my lord
Cardinal of York, are joined with me their servant,
In the unpartial judging of this business.

HENRY

Two equal men. The Queen shall be acquainted
Forthwith for what you come. Where's Gardiner?

WOLSEY

I know your Majesty has always loved her
So dear in heart, not to deny her that
A woman of less place might ask by law,
Scholars allowed freely to argue for her.

HENRY

Ay, and the best she shall have; and my favour
To him that does best, God forbid else. Cardinal,
Prithee call Gardiner to me, my new secretary:
I find him a fit fellow.

[*Exit Wolsey, and re-enter with Gardiner.*

WOLSEY [*aside to Gardiner*]

Give me your hand: much joy and favour to you,
You are the King's now.

Act two Scene two

GARDINER [*aside to Wolsey*]
> But to be commanded
For ever by your Grace, whose hand has raised
me.

HENRY
Come hither Gardiner.   [*Talks apart with him.*

CAMPEIUS
My Lord of York, was not one Doctor Pace
In this man's place before him?

WOLSEY
> Yes, he was.

CAMPEIUS
Was he not held a learned man?

WOLSEY
> Yes surely.

CAMPEIUS
Believe me, there's an ill opinion spread then,
Even of yourself Lord Cardinal.

WOLSEY
> How? Of me?

CAMPEIUS
They will not stick to say, you envied him;
And fearing he would rise, he was so virtuous,
Kept him a foreign man still; which so grieved him,
That he ran mad, and died.

WOLSEY
> Heaven's peace be with him.
That's Christian care enough; for living murmurers

There's places of rebuke. He was a fool;
For he would needs be virtuous. That good
 fellow,
If I command him, follows my appointment.
I will have none so near else. Learn this, brother, 135
We live not to be griped by meaner persons.
 HENRY
Deliver this with modesty to the Queen.
  [*Exit Gardiner.*
The most convenient place that I can think of
For such receipt of learning is Blackfriars;
There ye shall meet about this weighty business. 140
My Wolsey, see it furnished. O my lord,
Would it not grieve an able man to leave
So sweet a bedfellow? But conscience,
 conscience—
O 'tis a tender place, and I must leave her.
  [*Exeunt.*

Scene three

> *The same.   The Queen's antechamber.*
>
> *Enter Anne and Old Lady.*

ANNE
Not for that neither; here's the pang that pinches.
His Highness having lived so long with her, and
 she
So good a lady that no tongue could ever
Pronounce dishonour of her—by my life,

Act two Scene three 89

She never knew harm-doing—o, now after
So many courses of the sun enthroned,
Still growing in a majesty and pomp, the which
To leave a thousand-fold more bitter than
'Tis sweet at first t' acquire—after this process,
To give her the avaunt, it is a pity
Would move a monster.

OLD LADY
      Hearts of most hard temper
Melt and lament for her.

ANNE
      O God's will, much better
She ne'er had known pomp. Though't be temporal,
Yet if that quarrel, fortune, do divorce
It from the bearer, 'tis a sufferance, panging
As soul and body's severing.

OLD LADY
      Alas poor lady,
She's a stranger now again.

ANNE
      So much the more
Must pity drop upon her. Verily
I swear, 'tis better to be lowly born,
And range with humble livers in content,
Than to be perked up in a glistering grief,
And wear a golden sorrow.

OLD LADY
      Our content
Is our best having.

ANNE
>By my troth and maidenhead,
I would not be a queen.

OLD LADY
>Beshrew me, I would,
And venture maidenhead for't, and so would you,
For all this spice of your hypocrisy.
You that have so fair parts of woman on you,
Have too a woman's heart, which ever yet
Affected eminence, wealth, sovereignty;
Which, to say sooth, are blessings; and which gifts—
Saving your mincing—the capacity
Of your soft cheveril conscience would receive,
If you might please to stretch it.

ANNE
>Nay, good troth.

OLD LADY
Yes troth, and troth; you would not be a queen?

ANNE
No, not for all the riches under heaven.

OLD LADY
'Tis strange; a threepence bowed would hire me,
Old as I am, to queen it. But I pray you,
What think you of a duchess? Have you limbs
To bear that load of title?

ANNE
>No in truth.

OLD LADY
Then you are weakly made. Pluck off a little;

Act two Scene three

I would not be a young count in your way,
For more than blushing comes to. If your back
Cannot vouchsafe this burden, 'tis too weak
Ever to get a boy.

ANNE
           How you do talk.
I swear again, I would not be a queen,
For all the world.

OLD LADY
           In faith, for little England
You'd venture an emballing. I myself
Would for Carnarvonshire, although there longed
No more to the crown but that.
Enter Lord Chamberlain.
           Lo, who comes here?

LORD CHAMBERLAIN
Good morrow ladies; what were't worth to know
The secret of your conference?

ANNE
           My good lord,
Not your demand; it values not your asking.
Our mistress' sorrows we were pitying.

LORD CHAMBERLAIN
It was a gentle business, and becoming
The action of good women; there is hope
All will be well.

ANNE
           Now I pray God, amen.

LORD CHAMBERLAIN
You bear a gentle mind, and heavenly blessings

Follow such creatures. That you may, fair lady,
Perceive I speak sincerely, and high note's
Ta'en of your many virtues, the King's Majesty
Commends his good opinion of you to you, and
Does purpose honour to you no less flowing
Than Marchioness of Pembroke, to which title
A thousand pound a year, annual support,
Out of his grace he adds.

ANNE
                      I do not know
What kind of my obedience I should tender.
More than my all is nothing. Nor my prayers
Are not words duly hallowed, nor my wishes
More worth than empty vanities; yet prayers and wishes
Are all I can return. Beseech your lordship,
Vouchsafe to speak my thanks, and my obedience,
As from a blushing handmaid, to his Highness;
Whose health and royalty I pray for.

LORD CHAMBERLAIN
                          Lady,
I shall not fail t' approve the fair conceit
The King hath of you. [*Aside.*] I have perused her well;
Beauty and honour in her are so mingled,
That they have caught the King: and who knows yet
But from this lady may proceed a gem,

Act two Scene three 93

To lighten all the isle.—I'll to the King,
And say I spoke with you.
    ANNE
                    My honoured lord. 80
               [*Exit Lord Chamberlain.*
    OLD LADY
Why this it is. See, see,
I have been begging sixteen years in court,
Am yet a courtier beggarly, nor could
Come pat betwixt too early and too late
For any suit of pounds; and you, o fate, 85
A very fresh-fish here, fie, fie, fie upon
This compelled fortune, have your mouth filled up
Before you open it.
    ANNE
               This is strange to me.
    OLD LADY
How tastes it? Is it bitter? Forty pence, no.
There was a lady once—'tis an old story— 90
That would not be a queen, that would she not,
For all the mud in Egypt—have you heard it?
    ANNE
Come, you are pleasant.
    OLD LADY
                  With your theme, I could
O'ermount the lark. The Marchioness of Pembroke?
A thousand pounds a year, for pure respect? 95
No other obligation? By my life,

That promises moe thousands. Honour's train
Is longer than his foreskirt. By this time
I know your back will bear a duchess. Say,
Are you not stronger than you were?

    ANNE

                                Good lady, 100
Make yourself mirth with your particular fancy,
And leave me out on't. Would I had no being
If this salute my blood a jot; it faints me,
To think what follows.
The Queen is comfortless, and we forgetful 105
In our long absence: pray do not deliver
What here y'have heard to her.

    OLD LADY

                        What do you think me?
                                    [*Exeunt.*

Scene four

A hall in Blackfriars.

Trumpets, sennet, and cornets. Enter two Vergers, with short silver wands; next them two Scribes in the habit of Doctors and a Crier; after them, the Archbishop of Canterbury alone; after him, the Bishops of Lincoln, Ely, Rochester and Saint Asaph. Next them,

Act two Scene four 95

> *with some small distance, follows a Gentleman bearing the Purse, with the Great Seal, and a Cardinal's Hat. Then two Priests, bearing each a silver cross; then a Gentleman-Usher bare-headed, accompanied with a Sergeant-at-Arms bearing a silver mace; then two Gentlemen bearing two great silver pillars; after them, side by side, Wolsey and Campeius; two Noblemen with the sword and mace. Henry takes place under the cloth of state; Wolsey and Campeius sit under him as judges. Katherine, Griffith, and Attendants take place some distance from Henry. The Bishops place themselves on each side the court, in manner of a consistory; below them, the Scribes and Crier. The Lords sit next the Bishops. The rest of the Attendants stand in convenient order about the stage.*

WOLSEY
Whilst our commission from Rome is read,
Let silence be commanded.
　　　HENRY
　　　　　　　　　　What's the need?
It hath already publicly been read,
And on all sides the authority allowed;
You may then spare that time.

WOLSEY
                              Be't so, proceed.

SCRIBE
Say, Henry King of England, come into the
   court.

CRIER
Henry King of England, &c.

HENRY
Here.

SCRIBE
Say, Katherine Queen of England, come into
   the court.

CRIER
Katherine Queen of England, &c.

> [*Katherine makes no answer, rises out of
> her chair, goes about the court, comes to
> Henry, and kneels at his feet; then
> speaks.*

KATHERINE
Sir, I desire you do me right and justice,
And to bestow your pity on me: for
I am a most poor woman, and a stranger,
Born out of your dominions; having here
No judge indifferent, nor no more assurance
Of equal friendship and proceeding. Alas sir,
In what have I offended you? What cause
Hath my behaviour given to your displeasure,
That thus you should proceed to put me off,
And take your good grace from me? Heaven
   witness,

Act two Scene four

I have been to you a true and humble wife,
At all times to your will comformable;
Ever in fear to kindle your dislike, 25
Yea, subject to your countenance, glad, or sorry,
As I saw it inclined. When was the hour
I ever contradicted your desire?
Or made it not mine too? Or which of your friends
Have I not strove to love, although I knew 30
He were mine enemy? What friend of mine,
That had to him derived your anger, did I
Continue in my liking? Nay, gave notice
He was from thence discharged? Sir, call to mind
That I have been your wife, in this obedience, 35
Upward of twenty years, and have been blessed
With many children by you. If in the course
And process of this time, you can report,
And prove it too, against mine honour aught,
My bond to wedlock, or my love and duty, 40
Against your sacred person, in God's name,
Turn me away; and let the foul'st contempt
Shut door upon me, and so give me up
To the sharp'st kind of justice. Please you, sir,
The King you father was reputed for 45
A Prince most prudent, of an excellent
And unmatched wit and judgement. Ferdinand
My father, King of Spain, was reckoned one
The wisest Prince that there had reigned, by many

A year before. It is not to be questioned, 50
That they had gathered a wise council to them
Of every realm, that did debate this business,
Who deemed our marriage lawful. Wherefore I humbly
Beseech you sir, to spare me, till I may
Be by my friends in Spain advised; whose counsel 55
I will implore. If not, i' th' name of God,
Your pleasure be fulfilled.

    WOLSEY

                  You have here, lady,
And of your choice, these reverend fathers, men
Of singular integrity and learning,
Yea, the elect o' th' land, who are assembled 60
To plead your cause. It shall be therefore bootless
That longer you desire the court, as well
For your own quiet, as to rectify
What is unsettled in the King.

    CAMPEIUS

                  His Grace
Hath spoken well, and justly. Therefore madam, 65
It's fit this royal session do proceed,
And that, without delay, their arguments
Be now produced, and heard.

    KATHERINE

                  Lord Cardinal,
To you I speak.

Act two Scene four   99

WOLSEY
              Your pleasure, madam?
KATHERINE
                              Sir,
I am about to weep; but thinking that   70
We are a Queen, or long have dreamed so, certain
The daughter of a King, my drops of tears
I'll turn to sparks of fire.
WOLSEY
                    Be patient yet.
KATHERINE
I will, when you are humble; nay before,
Or God will punish me. I do believe,   75
Induced by potent circumstances, that
You are mine enemy, and make my challenge
You shall not be my judge. For it is you
Have blown this coal betwixt my lord and me,
Which God's dew quench; therefore, I say again,   80
I utterly abhor, yea, from my soul
Refuse you for my judge, whom yet once more
I hold my most malicious foe, and think not
At all a friend to truth.
WOLSEY
              I do profess
You speak not like yourself; who ever yet   85
Have stood to charity, and displayed the effects
Of disposition gentle, and of wisdom
O'ertopping woman's power. Madam, you do me wrong.

I have no spleen against you, nor injustice
For you, or any: how far I have proceeded,
Or how far further shall, is warranted
By a commission from the consistory,
Yea, the whole consistory of Rome. You charge me
That I have blown this coal: I do deny it.
The King is present. If it be known to him,
That I gainsay my deed, how may he wound,
And worthily, my falsehood, yea, as much
As you have done my truth. If he know
That I am free of your report, he knows
I am not of your wrong. Therefore in him
It lies to cure me, and the cure is to
Remove these thoughts from you. The which before
His Highness shall speak in, I do beseech
You, gracious madam, to unthink your speaking,
And to say so no more.

KATHERINE

               My lord, my lord,
I am a simple woman, much too weak
T' oppose your cunning. Y'are meek, and humble-mouthed;
You sign your place and calling, in full seeming,
With meekness and humility; but your heart
Is crammed with arrogancy, spleen, and pride.
You have by fortune, and his Highness' favours,
Gone slightly o'er low steps, and now are mounted

Act two Scene four

Where powers are your retainers, and your words,
Domestics to you, serve your will as't please
Yourself pronounce their office. I must tell you,
You tender more your person's honour than
Your high profession spiritual; that again
I do refuse you for my judge, and here
Before you all, appeal unto the Pope,
To bring my whole cause 'fore his Holiness,
And to be judged by him.

[*She curtsies to Henry and offers to depart.*

CAMPEIUS
                      The Queen is obstinate,
Stubborn to justice, apt to accuse it, and
Disdainful to be tried by't; 'tis not well.
She's going away.

HENRY
Call her again.

CRIER
Katherine Queen of England, come into the court.

GRIFFITH
Madam, you are called back.

KATHERINE
What need you note it? Pray you keep your way.
When you are called, return. Now, the Lord help,
They vex me past my patience. Pray you pass on.
I will not tarry; no, nor ever more

Upon this business my appearance make,
In any of their courts.
> [*Exeunt Katherine, Griffith, and Attendants.*

HENRY
                        Go thy ways Kate,
That man i' th' world who shall report he has
A better wife, let him in naught be trusted,   135
For speaking false in that; thou art alone,
If thy rare qualities, sweet gentleness,
Thy meekness saint-like, wife-like government,
Obeying in commanding, and thy parts
Sovereign and pious else, could speak thee out,   140
The queen of earthly queens. She's noble born;
And, like her true nobility, she has
Carried herself towards me.

WOLSEY
                        Most gracious sir,
In humblest manner I require your Highness,
That it shall please you to declare in hearing   145
Of all these ears, for where I am robbed and bound,
There must I be unloosed, although not there
At once and fully satisfied, whether ever I
Did broach this business to your Highness, or
Laid any scruple in your way which might   150
Induce you to the question on't; or ever
Have to you, but with thanks to God for such
A royal lady, spake one the least word that might

Act two Scene four

Be to the prejudice of her present state,
Or touch of her good person.

HENRY

                     My Lord Cardinal, 155
I do excuse you; yea, upon mine honour,
I free you from't. You are not to be taught
That you have many enemies, that know not
Why they are so, but like to village curs,
Bark when their fellows do. By some of these 160
The Queen is put in anger. Y'are excused.
But will you be more justified? You ever
Have wished the sleeping of this business, never
Desired it to be stirred; but oft have hindered, oft,
The passages made toward it; on my honour, 165
I speak my good Lord Cardinal to this point,
And thus far clear him. Now, what moved me to't,
I will be bold with time and your attention:
Then mark the inducement. Thus it came; give heed to't.
My conscience first received a tenderness, 170
Scruple, and prick, on certain speeches uttered
By th' Bishop of Bayonne, then French ambassador,
Who had been hither sent on the debating
A marriage 'twixt the Duke of Orleans and
Our daughter Mary. I' th' progress of this business, 175

Ere a determinate resolution, he—
I mean the bishop—did require a respite;
Wherein he might the King his lord advertise
Whether our daughter were legitimate,
Respecting this our marriage with the dowager, 180
Sometimes our brother's wife. This respite shook
The bosom of my conscience, entered me,
Yea, with a spitting power, and made to tremble
The region of my breast; which forced such way,
That many mazed considerings did throng, 185
And pressed in with this caution. First,
   methought
I stood not in the smile of heaven, who had
Commanded nature, that my lady's womb,
If it conceived a male child by me, should
Do no more offices of life to't than 190
The grave does to th' dead. For her male issue
Or died where they were made, or shortly after
This world had aired them. Hence I took a
   thought,
This was a judgement on me, that my kingdom,
Well worthy the best heir o' th' world, should
   not 195
Be gladded in't by me. Then follows, that
I weighed the danger which my realms stood in
By this my issue's fail, and that gave to me
Many a groaning throe. Thus hulling in
The wild sea of my conscience, I did steer 200
Toward this remedy, whereupon we are
Now present here together; that's to say,

Act two Scene four

I meant to rectify my conscience, which
I then did feel full sick, and yet not well,
By all the reverend fathers of the land, 205
And doctors learned. First I began in private
With you my Lord of Lincoln; you remember
How under my oppression I did reek,
When I first moved you.
   BISHOP OF LINCOLN
                    Very well my liege.
   HENRY
I have spoke long, be pleased yourself to say 210
How far you satisfied me.
   BISHOP OF LINCOLN
                    So please your Highness,
The question did at first so stagger me,
Bearing a state of mighty moment in't,
And consequence of dread, that I committed
The daring'st counsel which I had to doubt, 215
And did entreat your Highness to this course
Which you are running here.
   HENRY
                    I then moved you,
My Lord of Canterbury, and got your leave
To make this present summons: unsolicited
I left no reverend person in this court; 220
But by particular consent proceeded
Under your hands and seals; therefore go on,
For no dislike i' th' world against the person
Of the good Queen, but the sharp thorny points
Of my alleged reasons, drives this forward. 225

Prove but our marriage lawful, by my life
And kingly dignity, we are contented
To wear our mortal state to come, with her,
Katherine our Queen, before the primest creature
That's paragoned o' th' world.
    CAMPEIUS
                    So please your Highness,
The Queen being absent, 'tis a needful fitness,
That we adjourn this court till further day.
Meanwhile must be an earnest motion
Made to the Queen to call back her appeal
She intends unto his Holiness.
    HENRY [*aside*]
                      I may perceive
These Cardinals trifle with me. I abhor
This dilatory sloth, and tricks of Rome.
My learned and well beloved servant, Cranmer,
Prithee return. With thy approach, I know,
My comfort comes along. Break up the court:
I say, set on. [*Exeunt in the order of their entry.*

Act three Scene one

The palace. The Queen's chamber.

Katherine and her Women are discovered at work.

KATHERINE
Take thy lute wench; my soul grows sad with troubles.
Sing, and disperse 'em if thou canst; leave working.
　　A WOMAN [*sings*]
　Orpheus with his lute made trees,
　And the mountain tops that freeze,
　　　Bow themselves when he did sing. 5
　To his music, plants and flowers
　Ever sprung; as sun and showers
　　　There had made a lasting spring.

　Every thing that heard him play,
　Even the billows of the sea, 10
　　　Hung their heads, and then lay by.
　In sweet music is such art,

> Killing care, and grief of heart,
>   Fall asleep, or hearing die.

Enter Gentleman.

KATHERINE
How now?

GENTLEMAN
An't please your Grace, the two great Cardinals
Wait in the presence.

KATHERINE
                    Would they speak with me?

GENTLEMAN
They willed me say so madam.

KATHERINE
                    Pray their Graces
To come near. [*Exit Gentleman.*] What can be their business
With me, a poor weak woman, fallen from favour?
I do not like their coming, now I think on't.
They should be good men, their affairs as righteous;
But all hoods make not monks.

Enter Wolsey and Campeius.

WOLSEY
                    Peace to your Highness.

KATHERINE
Your Graces find me here part of a housewife;
I would be all, against the worst may happen.
What are your pleasures with me, reverend lords?

Act three Scene one

WOLSEY
May it please you noble madam, to withdraw
Into your private chamber, we shall give you
The full cause of our coming.

KATHERINE
                              Speak it here.
There's nothing I have done yet, o' my conscience,
Deserves a corner. Would all other women
Could speak this with as free a soul as I do.
My lords, I care not, so much I am happy
Above a number, if my actions
Were tried by every tongue, every eye saw 'em,
Envy and base opinion set against 'em,
I know my life so even. If your business
Seek me out, and that way I am wife in,
Out with it boldly. Truth loves open dealing.

WOLSEY
Tanta est erga te mentis integritas, Regina serenissima—

KATHERINE
O good my lord, no Latin;
I am not such a truant since my coming,
As not to know the language I have lived in.
A strange tongue makes my cause more strange, suspicious.
Pray speak in English; here are some will thank you,
If you speak truth, for their poor mistress' sake.

Believe me, she has had much wrong. Lord
   Cardinal,
The willing'st sin I ever yet committed
May be absolved in English.
   WOLSEY
                              Noble lady,
I am sorry my integrity should breed—
And service to his Majesty and you—
So deep suspicion, where all faith was meant.
We come not by the way of accusation,
To taint that honour every good tongue blesses,
Nor to betray you any way to sorrow;
You have too much good lady; but to know
How you stand minded in the weighty difference
Between the King and you, and to deliver,
Like free and honest men, our just opinions,
And comforts to your cause.
   CAMPEIUS
                         Most honoured madam,
My Lord of York, out of his noble nature,
Zeal and obedience he still bore your Grace,
Forgetting, like a good man, your late censure
Both of his truth and him, which was too far,
Offers, as I do, in a sign of peace,
His service and his counsel.
   KATHERINE [*aside*]
                         To betray me.—
My lords, I thank you both for your good wills;
Ye speak like honest men—pray God, ye prove
   so—

Act three Scene one

But how to make ye suddenly an answer,
In such a point of weight, so near mine honour—
More near my life I fear—with my weak wit,
And to such men of gravity and learning,
In truth I know not. I was set at work,
Among my maids, full little, God knows, looking
Either for such men, or such business.
For her sake that I have been—for I feel
The last fit of my greatness—good your Graces,
Let me have time and counsel for my cause.
Alas, I am a woman friendless, hopeless.

WOLSEY
Madam, you wrong the King's love with these fears.
Your hopes and friends are infinite.

KATHERINE
                              In England
But little for my profit. Can you think lords,
That any English man dare give me counsel?
Or be a known friend 'gainst his Highness' pleasure,
Though he be grown so desperate to be honest,
And live a subject? Nay forsooth, my friends,
They that must weigh out my afflictions,
They that my trust must grow to, live not here.
They are, as all my other comforts, far hence,
In mine own country, lords.

CAMPEIUS
                              I would your Grace
Would leave your griefs and take my counsel.

KATHERINE

                                            How sir?

CAMPEIUS

Put your main cause into the King's protection;
He's loving and most gracious. 'Twill be much
Both for your honour better, and your cause;   95
For if the trial of the law o'ertake ye,
You'll part away disgraced.

    WOLSEY

                           He tells you rightly.

KATHERINE

Ye tell me what ye wish for both, my ruin.
Is this your Christian counsel? Out upon ye!
Heaven is above all yet; there sits a Judge,   100
That no king can corrupt.

    CAMPEIUS

                         Your rage mistakes us.

KATHERINE

The more shame for ye; holy men I thought ye,
Upon my soul, two reverend cardinal virtues;
But cardinal sins, and hollow hearts I fear ye.
Mend 'em for shame my lords. Is this your comfort?   105
The cordial that ye bring a wretched lady,
A woman lost among ye, laughed at, scorned?
I will not wish ye half my miseries,
I have more charity. But say I warned ye;
Take heed, for heaven's sake take heed, lest at once   110
The burden of my sorrows fall upon ye.

Act three Scene one

WOLSEY
Madam, this is a mere distraction,
You turn the good we offer into envy.
KATHERINE
Ye turn me into nothing. Woe upon ye,
And all such false professors! Would you have me,
If you have any justice, any pity,
If ye be any thing but churchmen's habits,
Put my sick cause into his hands that hates me?
Alas, alas, has banished me his bed already,
His love, too long ago. I am old my lords,
And all the fellowship I hold now with him
Is only my obedience. What can happen
To me above this wretchedness? All your studies
Make me a curse like this.
CAMPEIUS
                              Your fears are worse.
KATHERINE
Have I lived thus long—let me speak myself,
Since virtue finds no friends—a wife, a true one?
A woman, I dare say without vainglory,
Never yet branded with suspicion?
Have I, with all my full affections
Still met the King? Loved him next heaven? Obeyed him?
Been, out of fondness, superstitious to him?
Almost forgot my prayers to content him?
And am I thus rewarded? 'Tis not well lords.

Bring me a constant woman to her husband,
One that ne'er dreamed a joy, beyond his
  pleasure;
And to that woman, when she has done most,
Yet will I add an honour, a great patience.
    WOLSEY
Madam, you wander from the good we aim at.
    KATHERINE
My lord, I dare not make myself so guilty,
To give up willingly that noble title
Your master wed me to; nothing but death
Shall e'er divorce my dignities.
    WOLSEY
                        Pray hear me.
    KATHERINE
Would I had never trod this English earth,
Or felt the flatteries that grow upon it.
Ye have angels' faces, but heaven knows your
  hearts.
What will become of me now, wretched lady?
I am the most unhappy woman living.
[*To her Women.*] Alas poor wenches, where are
  now your fortunes?
Shipwrecked upon a kingdom, where no pity,
No friends, no hope; no kindred weep for me;
Almost no grave allowed me. Like the lily,
That once was mistress of the field, and
  flourished,
I'll hang my head, and perish.

Act three Scene one

WOLSEY

If your Grace
Could but be brought to know our ends are honest,
You'd feel more comfort. Why should we, good lady,
Upon what cause wrong you? Alas, our places,
The way of our profession is against it;
We are to cure such sorrows, not to sow 'em.
For goodness' sake, consider what you do,
How you may hurt yourself, ay, utterly
Grow from the King's acquaintance, by this carriage.
The hearts of princes kiss obedience,
So much they love it. But to stubborn spirits,
They swell, and grow as terrible as storms.
I know you have a gentle, noble temper,
A soul as even as a calm: pray think us,
Those we profess, peace-makers, friends, and servants.

CAMPEIUS

Madam, you'll find it so. You wrong your virtues
With these weak women's fears. A noble spirit,
As yours was put into you, ever casts
Such doubts as false coin from it. The King loves you,
Beware you lose it not. For us, if you please
To trust us in your business, we are ready

To use our utmost studies in your service.
KATHERINE
Do what ye will, my lords. And pray forgive me, 175
If I have used myself unmannerly;
You know I am a woman, lacking wit
To make a seemly answer to such persons.
Pray do my service to his Majesty:
He has my heart yet, and shall have my prayers 180
While I shall have my life. Come reverend fathers,
Bestow your counsels on me. She now begs
That little thought, when she set footing here,
She should have bought her dignities so dear.
[*Exeunt.*

Scene two

The same. The King's antechamber.

Enter Norfolk, Suffolk, Surrey, and Lord Chamberlain.

NORFOLK
If you will now unite in your complaints,
And force them with a constancy, the Cardinal
Cannot stand under them. If you omit
The offer of this time, I cannot promise
But that you shall sustain moe new disgraces, 5

Act three Scene two

With these you bear already.
    SURREY

                    I am joyful
To meet the least occasion, that may give me
Remembrance of my father-in-law, the duke,
To be revenged on him.
    SUFFOLK

                      Which of the peers
Have uncontemned gone by him, or at least
Strangely neglected? When did he regard
The stamp of nobleness in any person
Out of himself?
    LORD CHAMBERLAIN

                My lords, you speak your pleasures.
What he deserves of you and me I know.
What we can do to him, though now the time
Gives way to us, I much fear. If you cannot
Bar his access to th' King, never attempt
Any thing on him; for he hath a witchcraft
Over the King in's tongue.
    NORFOLK

                      O fear him not,
His spell in that is out; the King hath found
Matter against him that for ever mars
The honey of his language. No, he's settled,
Not to come off, in his displeasure.
    SURREY

                            Sir,
I should be glad to hear such news as this
Once every hour.

NORFOLK
                    Believe it, this is true.
In the divorce, his contrary proceedings
Are all unfolded; wherein he appears
As I would wish mine enemy.
    SURREY
                            How came
His practices to light?
    SUFFOLK
                    Most strangely.
    SURREY
                                O, how, how?
    SUFFOLK
The Cardinal's letters to the Pope miscarried,
And came to th' eye o' th' King, wherein was read,
How that the Cardinal did entreat his Holiness
To stay the judgement o' th' divorce; for if
It did take place, I do, quoth he, perceive
My King is tangled in affection to
A creature of the Queen's, Lady Anne Bullen.
    SURREY
Has the King this?
    SUFFOLK
            Believe it.
    SURREY
                        Will this work?
    LORD CHAMBERLAIN
The King in this perceives him, how he coasts
And hedges his own way. But in this point

Act three Scene two

All his tricks founder, and he brings his physic
After his patient's death; the King already
Hath married the fair lady.
SURREY
                          Would he had.
SUFFOLK
May you be happy in your wish my lord,
For I profess you have it.
SURREY
                          Now all my joy
Trace the conjunction.
SUFFOLK
                    My amen to't.
NORFOLK
                              All men's.
SUFFOLK
There's order given for her coronation.
Marry this is yet but young, and may be left
To some ears unrecounted. But my lords,
She is a gallant creature, and complete
In mind and feature. I persuade me, from her
Will fall some blessing to this land, which shall
In it be memorized.
SURREY
              But will the King
Digest this letter of the Cardinal's?
The Lord forbid.
NORFOLK
          Marry amen.

SUFFOLK
                    No, no.
There be moe wasps that buzz about his nose
Will make this sting the sooner. Cardinal
    Campeius
Is stol'n away to Rome, hath ta'en no leave,
Has left the cause o' th' King unhandled, and
Is posted as the agent of our Cardinal,
To second all his plot. I do assure you,
The King cried ha at this.
        LORD CHAMBERLAIN
                        Now God incense him,
And let him cry ha louder.
        NORFOLK
                        But my lord,
When returns Cranmer?
        SUFFOLK
He is returned in his opinions, which
Have satisfied the King for his divorce,
Together with all famous colleges
Almost in Christendom; shortly, I believe,
His second marriage shall be published, and
Her coronation. Katherine no more
Shall be called Queen, but Princess Dowager
And widow to Prince Arthur.
        NORFOLK
                        This same Cranmer's
A worthy fellow, and hath ta'en much pain
In the King's business.

Act three Scene two

SUFFOLK
      He has, and we shall see him
For it an archbishop.
 NORFOLK
      So I hear.
 SUFFOLK
         'Tis so.

Enter Wolsey and Cromwell.

The Cardinal.
 NORFOLK
     Observe, observe, he's moody.
 WOLSEY
The packet Cromwell,
Gave't you the King?
 CROMWELL
     To his own hand, in's bedchamber.
 WOLSEY
Looked he o' th' inside of the paper?
 CROMWELL
         Presently
He did unseal them, and the first he viewed,
He did it with a serious mind; a heed
Was in his countenance. You he bade
Attend him here this morning.
 WOLSEY
        Is he ready
To come abroad?
 CROMWELL
   I think by this he is.

WOLSEY

Leave me awhile.   [*Exit Cromwell.*
It shall be to the Duchess of Alençon, 85
The French King's sister; he shall marry her.
Anne Bullen? No. I'll no Anne Bullens for him,
There's more in't than fair visage. Bullen?
No, we'll no Bullens. Speedily I wish
To hear from Rome. The Marchioness of
  Pembroke! 90

NORFOLK

He's discontented.

SUFFOLK

                     May be he hears the King
Does whet his anger to him.

SURREY

                              Sharp enough,
Lord, for thy justice.

WOLSEY

The late Queen's gentlewoman, a knight's
  daughter,
To be her mistress' mistress, the Queen's Queen? 95
This candle burns not clear, 'tis I must snuff it,
Then out it goes. What though I know her
  virtuous
And well deserving? Yet I know her for
A spleeny Lutheran, and not wholesome to
Our cause, that she should lie i' th' bosom of 100
Our hard-ruled King. Again, there is sprung up
An heretic, an arch one, Cranmer; one

Act three Scene two 123

Hath crawled into the favour of the King,
And is his oracle.
>   NORFOLK
>   He is vexed at something.
> *Enter Henry, reading a schedule, and Lovell.*
>   SURREY

I would 'twere something that would fret the string,
The master-cord on's heart.
>   SUFFOLK
>   The King, the King!
>   HENRY

What piles of wealth hath he accumulated
To his own portion! And what expense by th' hour
Seems to flow from him! How, i' th' name of thrift,
Does he rake this together? Now my lords,
Saw you the Cardinal?
>   NORFOLK
>   My lord, we have

Stood here observing him. Some strange commotion
Is in his brain. He bites his lip, and starts,
Stops on a sudden, looks upon the ground,
Then lays his finger on his temple; straight
Springs out into fast gait, then stops again,
Strikes his breast hard, and anon, he casts

His eye against the moon; in most strange
  postures
We have seen him set himself.
> HENRY

                       It may well be,
There is a mutiny in's mind. This morning,
Papers of state he sent me, to peruse
As I required; and wot you what I found
There—on my conscience, put unwittingly—
Forsooth an inventory, thus importing,
The several parcels of his plate, his treasure,
Rich stuffs and ornaments of household, which
I find at such proud rate, that it out-speaks
Possession of a subject.
> NORFOLK

                    It's heaven's will;
Some spirit put this paper in the packet,
To bless your eye withal.
> HENRY

                    If we did think
His contemplation were above the earth,
And fixed on spiritual object, he should still
Dwell in his musings, but I am afraid
His thinkings are below the moon, not worth
His serious considering.

> [*Takes his seat, whispers to Lovell, who
> brings Wolsey to Henry.*]
>
> WOLSEY

                  Heaven forgive me,
Ever God bless your Highness.

Act three Scene two

HENRY
                         Good my lord,
You are full of heavenly stuff, and bear the inventory
Of your best graces in your mind; the which
You were now running o'er. You have scarce time
To steal from spiritual leisure a brief span   140
To keep your earthly audit. Sure in that
I deem you an ill husband, and am glad
To have you therein my companion.
    WOLSEY
                              Sir,
For holy offices I have a time; a time
To think upon the part of business which   145
I bear i' th' state; and nature does require
Her times of preservation, which perforce
I her frail son, amongst my brethren mortal,
Must give my tendance to.
    HENRY
                        You have said well.
    WOLSEY
And ever may your Highness yoke together,   150
As I will lend you cause, my doing well
With my well saying.
    HENRY
                  'Tis well said again,
And 'tis a kind of good deed to say well,
And yet words are no deeds. My father loved you;
He said he did, and with his deed did crown   155

His word upon you. Since I had my office,
I have kept you next my heart, have not alone
Employed you where high profits might come home,
But pared my present havings, to bestow
My bounties upon you.

  WOLSEY [*aside*]
        What should this mean? 160
  SURREY [*aside*]
The Lord increase this business.
  HENRY
        Have I not made you
The prime man of the state? I pray you tell me,
If what I now pronounce you have found true.
And if you may confess it, say withal
If you are bound to us, or no. What say you? 165
  WOLSEY
My sovereign, I confess your royal graces,
Showered on me daily, have been more than could
My studied purposes requite, which went
Beyond all man's endeavours. My endeavours
Have ever come too short of my desires, 170
Yet filled with my abilities. Mine own ends
Have been mine so, that evermore they pointed
To th' good of your most sacred person, and
The profit of the state. For your great graces
Heaped upon me, poor undeserver, I 175
Can nothing render but allegiant thanks,
My prayers to heaven for you, my loyalty,

Act three Scene two

Which ever has, and ever shall be growing,
Till death, that winter, kill it.
    HENRY
                        Fairly answered.
A loyal and obedient subject is
Therein illustrated; the honour of it
Does pay the act of it, as i' th' contrary
The foulness is the punishment. I presume,
That as my hand has opened bounty to you,
My heart dropped love, my power rained honour, more
On you than any; so your hand, and heart,
Your brain, and every function of your power,
Should, notwithstanding that your bond of duty,
As 'twere in love's particular, be more
To me your friend, than any.
    WOLSEY
                        I do profess,
That for your Highness' good I ever laboured
More than mine own; that am, have, and will be—
Though all the world should crack their duty to you,
And throw it from their soul, though perils did
Abound, as thick as thought could make 'em, and
Appear in forms more horrid—yet my duty,
As doth a rock against the chiding flood,
Should the approach of this wild river break,
And stand unshaken yours.

HENRY

                'Tis nobly spoken.
Take notice lords, he has a loyal breast,
For you have seen him open't. Read o'er this;
       [*Gives him papers.*
And after, this, and then to breakfast with
What appetite you have.
   [*Exit Henry, frowning upon Wolsey:
   the Nobles throng after him, smiling and
   whispering.*

WOLSEY

              What should this mean?
What sudden anger's this? How have I reaped it?
He parted frowning from me, as if ruin
Leaped from his eyes. So looks the chafed lion
Upon the daring huntsman that has galled him;
Then makes him nothing. I must read this paper;
I fear, the story of his anger. 'Tis so.
This paper has undone me. 'Tis th' accompt
Of all that world of wealth I have drawn together
For mine own ends, indeed to gain the Popedom,
And fee my friends in Rome. O negligence,
Fit for a fool to fall by! What cross devil
Made me put this main secret in the packet
I sent the King? Is there no way to cure this?
No new device to beat this from his brains?
I know 'twill stir him strongly; yet I know
A way, if it take right, in spite of fortune
Will bring me off again. What's this? *To th' Pope?*
The letter, as I live, with all the business

Act three Scene two

I writ to's Holiness. Nay then, farewell.
I have touched the highest point of all my greatness,
And from that full meridian of my glory,
I haste now to my setting. I shall fall
Like a bright exhalation in the evening,
And no man see me more.

Enter Norfolk, Suffolk, Surrey, and Lord Chamberlain.

NORFOLK

Hear the King's pleasure Cardinal, who commands you
To render up the Great Seal presently
Into our hands, and to confine yourself
To Asher House, my Lord of Winchester's,
Till you hear further from his Highness.

WOLSEY
                                    Stay.
Where's your commission, lords? Words cannot carry
Authority so weighty.

SUFFOLK
                    Who dare cross 'em,
Bearing the King's will from his mouth expressly?

WOLSEY

Till I find more than will or words to do it,
I mean your malice, know, officious lords,
I dare, and must deny it. Now I feel
Of what coarse metal ye are moulded, envy;
How eagerly ye follow my disgraces

As if it fed ye, and how sleek and wanton
Ye appear in every thing may bring my ruin.
Follow your envious courses, men of malice;
You have Christian warrant for 'em, and no doubt
In time will find their fit rewards. That Seal 245
You ask with such a violence, the King,
Mine and your master, with his own hand gave me;
Bade me enjoy it, with the place, and honours,
During my life; and, to confirm his goodness,
Tied it by letters patents. Now, who'll take it? 250
   SURREY
The King that gave it.
   WOLSEY
              It must be himself then.
   SURREY
Thou art a proud traitor, priest.
   WOLSEY
              Proud lord, thou liest.
Within these forty hours, Surrey durst better
Have burnt that tongue then said so.
   SURREY
              Thy ambition,
Thou scarlet sin, robbed this bewailing land 255
Of noble Buckingham, my father-in-law.
The heads of all thy brother Cardinals,
With thee and all thy best parts bound together,
Weighed not a hair of his. Plague of your policy!

Act three Scene two

You sent me deputy for Ireland,
Far from his succour, from the King, from all
That might have mercy on the fault thou gavest
   him;
Whilst your great goodness, out of holy pity,
Absolved him with an axe.
    WOLSEY
                      This, and all else
This talking lord can lay upon my credit,
I answer is most false. The duke by law
Found his deserts. How innocent I was
From any private malice in his end,
His noble jury, and foul cause can witness.
If I loved many words, lord, I should tell you
You have as little honesty as honour,
That in the way of loyalty and truth
Toward the King, my ever royal master,
Dare mate a sounder man than Surrey can be,
And all that love his follies.
    SURREY
                      By my soul,
Your long coat, priest, protects you; thou
   shouldst feel
My sword i' th' life-blood of thee else. My lords,
Can ye endure to hear this arrogance?
And from this fellow? If we live thus tamely,
To be thus jaded by a piece of scarlet,
Farewell nobility; let his Grace go forward,
And dare us with his cap like larks.

WOLSEY

                              All goodness
Is poison to thy stomach.

SURREY

                    Yes, that goodness
Of gleaning all the land's wealth into one,
Into your own hands, Cardinal, by extortion;
The goodness of your intercepted packets
You writ to th' Pope against the King; your goodness,
Since you provoke me, shall be most notorious.
My Lord of Norfolk, as you are truly noble,
As you respect the common good, the state
Of our despised nobility, our issues,
Whom, if he live, will scarce be gentlemen,
Produce the grand sum of his sins, the articles
Collected from his life. I'll startle you
Worse than the sacring bell, when the brown wench
Lay kissing in your arms, Lord Cardinal.

WOLSEY

How much methinks I could despise this man,
But that I am bound in charity against it.

NORFOLK

Those articles, my lord, are in the King's hand;
But thus much, they are foul ones.

WOLSEY

                              So much fairer
And spotless shall mine innocence arise,
When the King knows my truth.

Act three Scene two

SURREY

                       This cannot save you.
I thank my memory, I yet remember
Some of these articles, and out they shall.
Now, if you can blush, and cry guilty, Cardinal,
You'll show a little honesty.

WOLSEY

                       Speak on sir,
I dare your worst objections. If I blush,
It is to see a nobleman want manners.

SURREY

I had rather want those, than my head; have at you.
First, that without the King's assent or knowledge,
You wrought to be a Legate, by which power
You maimed the jurisdiction of all bishops.

NORFOLK

Then, that in all you writ to Rome, or else
To foreign princes, *Ego et Rex meus*
Was still inscribed; in which you brought the King
To be your servant.

SUFFOLK

                     Then, that without the knowledge
Either of King or Council, when you went
Ambassador to the Emperor, you made bold
To carry into Flanders the Great Seal.

SURREY

Item, you sent a large commission

To Gregory de Cassado, to conclude
Without the King's will, or the state's allowance,
A league between his Highness and Ferrara.
  SUFFOLK
That out of mere ambition, you have caused
Your holy hat to be stamped on the King's coin. 325
  SURREY
Then, that you have sent innumerable substance—
By what means got, I leave to your own conscience—
To furnish Rome, and to prepare the ways
You have for dignities, to the mere undoing
Of all the kingdom. Many more there are, 330
Which since they are of you, and odious,
I will not taint my mouth with.
  LORD CHAMBERLAIN
        O my lord,
Press not a falling man too far; 'tis virtue.
His faults lie open to the laws; let them,
Not you, correct him. My heart weeps to see him 335
So little of his great self.
  SURREY
        I forgive him.
  SUFFOLK
Lord Cardinal, the King's further pleasure is,
Because all those things you have done of late
By your power legatine within this kingdom,
Fall into th' compass of a praemunire, 340

Act three Scene two

That therefore such a writ be sued against you,
To forfeit all your goods, lands, tenements,
Chattels, and whatsoever, and to be
Out of the King's protection. This is my charge.
>NORFOLK

And so we'll leave you to your meditations 345
How to live better. For your stubborn answer
About the giving back the Great Seal to us,
The King shall know it, and, no doubt, shall
  thank you.
So fare you well, my little good Lord Cardinal.
>[*Exeunt all but Wolsey.*
>WOLSEY

So farewell—to the little good you bear me. 350
Farewell? A long farewell to all my greatness.
This is the state of man: to-day he puts forth
The tender leaves of hope; to-morrow blossoms,
And bears his blushing honours thick upon him;
The third day comes a frost, a killing frost, 355
And when he thinks, good easy man, full surely
His greatness is a-ripening, nips his root,
And then he falls as I do. I have ventured
Like little wanton boys that swim on bladders,
This many summers in a sea of glory, 360
But far beyond my depth. My high-blown pride
At length broke under me, and now has left me,
Weary, and old with service, to the mercy
Of a rude stream, that must for ever hide me.
Vain pomp, and glory of this world, I hate ye; 365
I feel my heart new opened. O how wretched

Is that poor man that hangs on princes' favours!
There is betwixt that smile we would aspire to,
That sweet aspect of princes, and their ruin,
More pangs and fears than wars or women have; 370
And when he falls, he falls like Lucifer,
Never to hope again.
    Enter Cromwell.
                    Why how now Cromwell!
    CROMWELL
I have no power to speak sir.
    WOLSEY
                    What, amazed
At my misfortunes? Can thy spirit wonder
A great man should decline? Nay, an you weep 375
I am fallen indeed.
    CROMWELL
                How does your Grace?
    WOLSEY
                                Why well;
Never so truly happy, my good Cromwell.
I know myself now, and I feel within me
A peace above all earthly dignities,
A still and quiet conscience. The King has cured me, 380
I humbly thank his Grace; and from these shoulders,
These ruined pillars, out of pity, taken
A load would sink a navy—too much honour.

Act three Scene two

O, 'tis a burden Cromwell, 'tis a burden
Too heavy for a man that hopes for heaven.   385

CROMWELL

I am glad your Grace has made that right use of it.

WOLSEY

I hope I have. I am able now, methinks,
Out of a fortitude of soul I feel,
To endure more miseries and greater far
Than my weak-hearted enemies dare offer.   390
What news abroad?

CROMWELL

                 The heaviest, and the worst,
Is your displeasure with the King.

WOLSEY

                               God bless him.

CROMWELL

The next is, that Sir Thomas More is chosen
Lord Chancellor, in your place.

WOLSEY

                       That's somewhat sudden
But he's a learned man. May he continue   395
Long in his Highness' favour, and do justice
For truth's sake and his conscience; that his bones,
When he has run his course, and sleeps in blessings,
May have a tomb of orphans' tears wept on him.
What more?

CROMWELL
    That Cranmer is returned with welcome,
Installed Lord Archbishop of Canterbury.
WOLSEY
That's news indeed.
CROMWELL
            Last, that the Lady Anne,
Whom the King hath in secrecy long married,
This day was viewed in open, as his Queen,
Going to chapel; and the voice is now
Only about her coronation.
WOLSEY
There was the weight that pulled me down. O Cromwell,
The King has gone beyond me. All my glories
In that one woman I have lost for ever.
No sun shall ever usher forth mine honours,
Or gild again the noble troops that waited
Upon my smiles. Go get thee from me Cromwell,
I am a poor fallen man, unworthy now
To be thy lord and master. Seek the King.
That sun I pray may never set. I have told him
What, and how true thou art; he will advance thee.
Some little memory of me will stir him—
I know his noble nature—not to let
Thy hopeful service perish too. Good Cromwell,
Neglect him not; make use now, and provide
For thine own future safety.

Act three Scene two

CROMWELL

                O my lord,
Must I then leave you? Must I needs forgo
So good, so noble, and so true a master?
Bear witness, all that have not hearts of iron,
With what a sorrow Cromwell leaves his lord. 425
The King shall have my service; but my prayers
For ever and for ever shall be yours.

WOLSEY

Cromwell, I did not think to shed a tear
In all my miseries; but thou hast forced me,
Out of thy honest truth, to play the woman. 430
Let's dry our eyes; and thus far hear me
   Cromwell;
And when I am forgotten, as I shall be,
And sleep in dull cold marble, where no mention
Of me more must be heard of—say I taught
   thee—
Say, Wolsey, that once trod the ways of glory, 435
And sounded all the depths and shoals of honour,
Found thee a way, out of his wreck, to rise in;
A sure and safe one, though thy master missed it.
Mark but my fall, and that that ruined me.
Cromwell, I charge thee, fling away ambition. 440
By that sin fell the angels; how can man then,
The image of his Maker, hope to win by it?
Love thyself last, cherish those hearts that hate
   thee;
Corruption wins not more than honesty.

Still in thy right hand carry gentle peace, 445
To silence envious tongues. Be just, and fear not;
Let all the ends thou aim'st at be thy country's,
Thy God's, and truth's. Then if thou fall'st, o Cromwell,
Thou fall'st a blessed martyr. Serve the King;
And prithee lead me in. 450
There take an inventory of all I have,
To the last penny, 'tis the King's. My robe,
And my integrity to heaven, is all
I dare now call mine own. O Cromwell, Cromwell,
Had I but served my God, with half the zeal 455
I served my King, he would not in mine age
Have left me naked to mine enemies.

  CROMWELL
Good sir, have patience.
  WOLSEY
      So I have. Farewell
The hopes of Court, my hopes in heaven do dwell.

       [*Exeunt.*

Act four Scene one

A street in Westminster.

Enter two Gentlemen, at several doors, meeting.

FIRST GENTLEMAN
Y'are well met once again.
　　SECOND GENTLEMAN
　　　　　　　　So are you.
　　FIRST GENTLEMAN
You come to take your stand here, and behold
The Lady Anne pass from her coronation?
　　SECOND GENTLEMAN
'Tis all my business. At our last encounter
The Duke of Buckingham came from his trial.
　　FIRST GENTLEMAN
'Tis very true. But that time offered sorrow,
This general joy.
　　SECOND GENTLEMAN
　　　　　　'Tis well: the citizens
I am sure have shown at full their royal minds,

142   *King Henry the Eighth*

As, let 'em have their rights, they are ever
  forward,
In celebration of this day with shows,
Pageants, and sights of honour.
    FIRST GENTLEMAN
                              Never greater,
Nor, I'll assure you, better taken sir.
    SECOND GENTLEMAN
May I be bold to ask what that contains,
That paper in your hand?
    FIRST GENTLEMAN
                        Yes, 'tis the list
Of those that claim their offices this day,
By custom of the coronation.
The Duke of Suffolk is the first, and claims
To be High Steward; next, the Duke of Norfolk,
He to be Earl Marshal: you may read the rest.
    SECOND GENTLEMAN
I thank you sir: had I not known those customs,
I should have been beholding to your paper.
But I beseech you, what's become of Katherine,
The Princess Dowager? How goes her business?
    FIRST GENTLEMAN
That I can tell you too. The Archbishop
Of Canterbury, accompanied with other
Learned and reverend fathers of his order,
Held a late court at Dunstable, six miles off
From Ampthill, where the Princess lay; to which
She was often cited by them, but appeared not:
And to be short, for not appearance, and

Act four Scene one

The King's late scruple, by the main assent
Of all these learned men, she was divorced,
And the late marriage made of none effect;
Since which she was removed to Kimbolton,
Where she remains now sick.

SECOND GENTLEMAN

                    Alas good lady! [*Trumpets.*
The trumpets sound. Stand close, the Queen is coming.   [*Hautboys.*

THE ORDER OF THE CORONATION

1. *A lively flourish of trumpets.*
2. *Then, two Judges.*
3. *Lord Chancellor, with purse and mace before him.*
4. *Choristers singing.*   [*Music.*
5. *Mayor of London, bearing the mace. Then Garter, in his coat of arms, and on his head he wore a gilt copper crown.*
6. *Marquess Dorset, bearing a sceptre of gold, on his head a demi-coronal of gold. With him, the Earl of Surrey, bearing the rod of silver with the dove, crowned with an earl's coronet. Collars of esses.*
7. *Duke of Suffolk, in his robe of estate, his coronet on his head, bearing a long white wand, as High Steward. With him, the Duke of Norfolk, with the rod of marshalship, a coronet on his head. Collars of esses.*
8. *A canopy borne by four of the Cinque Ports, under it Anne in her robe, in her hair*

> *richly adorned with pearl, crowned. On each side her, the Bishops of London, and Winchester.*
> 9. *The old Duchess of Norfolk, in a coronal of gold, wrought with flowers, bearing Anne's train.*
> 10. *Certain Ladies or Countesses, with plain circlets of gold without flowers.*
>> *Exeunt, first passing over the stage in order and state, and then, a great flourish of trumpets.*

A royal train, believe me. These I know.
Who's that that bears the sceptre?

FIRST GENTLEMAN
                      Marquess Dorset,
And that the Earl of Surrey, with the rod.

SECOND GENTLEMAN
A bold brave gentleman. That should be
The Duke of Suffolk.

FIRST GENTLEMAN
              'Tis the same: High Steward.

SECOND GENTLEMAN
And that my Lord of Norfolk?

FIRST GENTLEMAN
                    Yes.

SECOND GENTLEMAN [*looks on Anne*]
                  Heaven bless thee,
Thou hast the sweetest face I ever looked on.
Sir, as I have a soul, she is an angel;
Our King has all the Indies in his arms,

Act four Scene one

And more, and richer, when he strains that lady.
I cannot blame his conscience.
   FIRST GENTLEMAN
                              They that bear
The cloth of honour over her are four Barons
Of the Cinque Ports.
   SECOND GENTLEMAN
Those men are happy, and so are all are near her.
I take it, she that carries up the train
Is that old noble lady, Duchess of Norfolk?
   FIRST GENTLEMAN
It is, and all the rest are countesses.
   SECOND GENTLEMAN
Their coronets say so. These are stars indeed,
And sometimes falling ones.
   FIRST GENTLEMAN
                              No more of that.
Enter Third Gentleman.
God save you sir. Where have you been broiling?
   THIRD GENTLEMAN
Among the crowd i' th' Abbey, where a finger
Could not be wedged in more. I am stifled
With the mere rankness of their joy.
   SECOND GENTLEMAN
                              You saw
The ceremony?
   THIRD GENTLEMAN
        That I did.

FIRST GENTLEMAN
                How was it?
THIRD GENTLEMAN
Well worth the seeing.
        SECOND GENTLEMAN
                        Good sir, speak it to us.
    THIRD GENTLEMAN
As well as I am able. The rich stream
Of lords and ladies, having brought the Queen
To a prepared place in the choir, fell off
A distance from her; while her Grace sat down
To rest awhile, some half an hour or so,
In a rich chair of state, opposing freely
The beauty of her person to the people.
Believe me sir, she is the goodliest woman
That ever lay by man; which when the people
Had the full view of, such a noise arose
As the shrouds make at sea, in a stiff tempest,
As loud, and to as many tunes. Hats, cloaks—
Doublets, I think—flew up, and had their faces
Been loose, this day they had been lost. Such joy
I never saw before. Great-bellied women,
That had not half a week to go, like rams
In the old time of war, would shake the press,
And make 'em reel before 'em. No man living
Could say, this is my wife, there, all were woven
So strangely in one piece.
        SECOND GENTLEMAN
                        But what followed?

Act four Scene one   147
THIRD GENTLEMAN
At length, her Grace rose, and with modest paces
Came to the altar, where she kneeled, and saint-like
Cast her fair eyes to heaven, and prayed devoutly,
Then rose again, and bowed her to the people;   85
When by the Archbishop of Canterbury,
She had all the royal makings of a queen;
As holy oil, Edward Confessor's crown,
The rod, and bird of peace, and all such emblems
Laid nobly on her; which performed, the choir,   90
With all the choicest music of the kingdom,
Together sung Te Deum. So she parted,
And with the same full state paced back again
To York Place, where the feast is held.
FIRST GENTLEMAN
                           Sir,
You must no more call it York Place, that's past;   95
For since the Cardinal fell, that title's lost.
'Tis now the King's, and called Whitehall.
THIRD GENTLEMAN
                       I know it;
But 'tis so lately altered, that the old name
Is fresh about me.
SECOND GENTLEMAN
               What two reverend bishops
Were those that went on each side of the Queen?   100

THIRD GENTLEMAN
Stokesly and Gardiner, the one of Winchester,
Newly preferred from the King's secretary;
The other London.
SECOND GENTLEMAN
He of Winchester
Is held no great good lover of the archbishop's,
The virtuous Cranmer.
THIRD GENTLEMAN
All the land knows that.
However, yet there is no great breach; when it comes,
Cranmer will find a friend will not shrink from him.
SECOND GENTLEMAN
Who may that be, I pray you?
THIRD GENTLEMAN
Thomas Cromwell,
A man in much esteem with the King, and truly
A worthy friend. The King
Has made him master o' th' Jewel House,
And one already of the Privy Council.
SECOND GENTLEMAN
He will deserve more.
THIRD GENTLEMAN
Yes, without all doubt.
Come gentlemen, ye shall go my way, which
Is to th' Court, and there ye shall be my guests.
Something I can command. As I walk thither,
I'll tell ye more.

Act four Scene one

BOTH
You may command us sir. [*Exeunt.*

Scene two

Kimbolton.

Enter Katherine, supported by Griffith and Patience.

GRIFFITH
How does your Grace?
KATHERINE
O Griffith, sick to death.
My legs like loaden branches bow to th' earth,
Willing to leave their burden. Reach a chair.
So, now, methinks, I feel a little ease.
Didst thou not tell me Griffith, as thou led'st me,
That the great child of honour, Cardinal Wolsey,
Was dead?
GRIFFITH
Yes madam; but I think your Grace,
Out of the pain you suffered, gave no ear to't.
KATHERINE
Prithee good Griffith, tell me how he died.
If well, he stepped before me happily

For my example.
>   GRIFFITH
>   Well, the voice goes madam;
> For after the stout Earl Northumberland
> Arrested him at York, and brought him forward,
> As a man sorely tainted, to his answer,
> He fell sick suddenly, and grew so ill   15
> He could not sit his mule.
>   KATHERINE
>   Alas poor man!
>   GRIFFITH
> At last, with easy roads, he came to Leicester,
> Lodged in the abbey; where the reverend abbot
> With all his covent honourably received him;
> To whom he gave these words, o Father Abbot,   20
> An old man, broken with the storms of state,
> Is come to lay his weary bones among ye;
> Give him a little earth for charity.
> So went to bed; where eagerly his sickness
> Pursued him still; and three nights after this,   25
> About the hour of eight, which he himself
> Foretold should be his last, full of repentance,
> Continual meditations, tears, and sorrows,
> He gave his honours to the world again,
> His blessed part to heaven, and slept in peace.   30
>   KATHERINE
> So may he rest; his faults lie gently on him.
> Yet thus far Griffith, give me leave to speak him,
> And yet with charity. He was a man
> Of an unbounded stomach, ever ranking

Himself with princes; one that by suggestion
Tied all the kingdom. Simony was fair play;
His own opinion was his law. I' th' presence
He would say untruths, and be ever double
Both in his words, and meaning. He was never,
But where he meant to ruin, pitiful.
His promises were, as he then was, mighty;
But his performance, as he is now, nothing.
Of his own body he was ill, and gave
The clergy ill example.

GRIFFITH

Noble madam,
Men's evil manners live in brass; their virtues
We write in water. May it please your Highness
To hear me speak his good now?

KATHERINE

Yes good Griffith,
I were malicious else.

GRIFFITH

This Cardinal,
Though from an humble stock, undoubtedly
Was fashioned to much honour. From his cradle.
He was a scholar, and a ripe and good one;
Exceeding wise, fair-spoken, and persuading;
Lofty and sour to them that loved him not,
But to those men that sought him sweet as summer.
And though he were unsatisfied in getting,
Which was a sin, yet in bestowing, madam,
He was most princely; ever witness for him

Those twins of learning that he raised in you,
Ipswich and Oxford, one of which fell with him,
Unwilling to outlive the good that did it; 60
The other, though unfinished, yet so famous,
So excellent in art, and still so rising,
That Christendom shall ever speak his virtue.
His overthrow heaped happiness upon him;
For then, and not till then, he felt himself, 65
And found the blessedness of being little.
And to add greater honours to his age
Than man could give him, he died, fearing God.

KATHERINE
After my death, I wish no other herald,
No other speaker of my living actions, 70
To keep mine honour from corruption,
But such an honest chronicler as Griffith.
Whom I most hated living, thou hast made me,
With thy religious truth and modesty,
Now in his ashes honour. Peace be with him. 75
Patience, be near me still, and set me lower.
I have not long to trouble thee. Good Griffith,
Cause the musicians play me that sad note
I named my knell, whilst I sit meditating
On that celestial harmony I go to. 80

[*Sad and solemn music.*

GRIFFITH
She is asleep. Good wench, let's sit down quiet,
For fear we wake her. Softly, gentle Patience.

The Vision
Enter solemnly tripping one after an-

Act four Scene two

other, six personages, clad in white robes, wearing on their heads garlands of bays, and golden vizards on their faces, branches of bays or palm in their hands. They first congee unto her, then dance; and at certain changes, the first two hold a spare garland over her head, at which the other four make reverent curtsies. Then the two that held the garland deliver the same to the other next two, who observe the same order in their changes, and holding the garland over her head. Which done, they deliver the same garland to the last two, who likewise observe the same order. At which (as it were by inspiration) she makes (in her sleep) signs of rejoicing and holdeth up her hands to heaven. And so, in their dancing vanish, carrying the garland with them. The music continues.

KATHERINE
Spirits of peace, where are ye? Are ye all gone,
And leave me here in wretchedness behind ye?

GRIFFITH
Madam, we are here.

KATHERINE
     It is not you I call for. 85
Say ye none enter since I slept?

GRIFFITH

                      None madam.

KATHERINE

No? Saw you not even now a blessed troop
Invite me to a banquet, whose bright faces
Cast thousand beams upon me, like the sun?
They promised me eternal happiness,
And brought me garlands, Griffith, which I feel
I am not worthy yet to wear. I shall
Assuredly.

GRIFFITH

I am most joyful madam, such good dreams
Possess your fancy.

KATHERINE

                Bid the music leave,
They are harsh and heavy to me. [*Music ceases.*

PATIENCE

                        Do you note
How much her Grace is altered on the sudden?
How long her face is drawn? How pale she looks,
And of an earthy cold? Mark her eyes.

GRIFFITH

She is going wench. Pray, pray.

PATIENCE

                      Heaven comfort her.

Enter Messenger.

MESSENGER

An't like your Grace—

KATHERINE

                You are a saucy fellow,

Act four Scene two

Deserve we no more reverence?
GRIFFITH
You are to blame,
Knowing she will not lose her wonted greatness,
To use so rude behaviour. Go to, kneel.
MESSENGER
I humbly do entreat your Highness' pardon;
My haste made me unmannerly. There is staying
A gentleman, sent from the King, to see you.
KATHERINE
Admit him entrance Griffith. But this fellow
Let me ne'er see again.   [*Exit Messenger.*
Enter Capuchius.
If my sight fail not,
You should be Lord Ambassador from the Emperor,
My royal nephew, and your name Capuchius.
CAPUCHIUS
Madam the same. Your servant.
KATHERINE
O my lord,
The times and titles now are altered strangely
With me, since first you knew me. But I pray you,
What is your pleasure with me?
CAPUCHIUS
Noble lady,
First mine own service to your Grace, the next
The King's request, that I would visit you;
Who grieves much for your weakness, and by me

Sends you his princely commendations,
And heartily entreats you take good comfort.
KATHERINE
O my good lord, that comfort comes too late, 120
'Tis like a pardon after execution;
That gentle physic, given in time, had cured me.
But now I am past all comforts here, but
  prayers.
How does his Highness?
CAPUCHIUS
              Madam, in good health.
KATHERINE
So may he ever do, and ever flourish, 125
When I shall dwell with worms, and my poor
  name
Banished the kingdom. Patience, is that letter
I caused you write yet sent away?
PATIENCE
                  No madam.
          [*Gives it to Katherine.*
KATHERINE
Sir, I most humbly pray you to deliver
This to my lord the King.
CAPUCHIUS
                Most willing madam. 130
KATHERINE
In which I have commended to his goodness
The model of our chaste loves, his young
  daughter—

Act four Scene two

The dews of heaven fall thick in blessings on
  her—
Beseeching him to give her virtuous breeding;
She is young, and of a noble modest nature; 135
I hope she will deserve well; and a little
To love her for her mother's sake, that loved
  him,
Heaven knows how dearly. My next poor
  petition
Is, that his noble Grace would have some pity
Upon my wretched women, that so long 140
Have followed both my fortunes faithfully,
Of which there is not one, I dare avow,
And now I should not lie, but will deserve,
For virtue, and true beauty of the soul,
For honesty and decent carriage, 145
A right good husband, let him be a noble;
And sure those men are happy that shall have
  'em.
The last is for my men, they are the poorest,
But poverty could never draw 'em from me,
That they may have their wages duly paid 'em, 150
And something over to remember me by.
If heaven had pleased to have given me longer
  life
And able means, we had not parted thus.
These are the whole contents; and good my lord,
By that you love the dearest in this world, 155
As you wish Christian peace to souls departed,

Stand these poor people's friend, and urge the King
To do me this last right.
CAPUCHIUS
By heaven I will,
Or let me lose the fashion of a man.
KATHERINE
I thank you honest lord. Remember me 160
In all humility unto his Highness.
Say his long trouble now is passing
Out of this world. Tell him in death I blessed him,
For so I will. Mine eyes grow dim. Farewell
My lord. Griffith farewell. Nay Patience, 165
You must not leave me yet. I must to bed;
Call in more women. When I am dead, good wench,
Let me be used with honour; strew me over
With maiden flowers, that all the world may know
I was a chaste wife, to my grave. Embalm me, 170
Then lay me forth; although unqueened, yet like
A Queen, and daughter to a King inter me.
I can no more.   [*Exeunt, leading Katherine.*

Act five Scene one

London. A gallery in the palace.

Enter at one door Gardiner, and Page before him with a torch.

GARDINER
It's one a clock boy, is't not?
　　PAGE
　　　　　　　　　It hath struck.
GARDINER
These should be hours for necessities,
Not for delights; times to repair our nature
With comforting repose, and not for us
To waste these times.
　　Enter Lovell at the other door.
　　　　　Good hour of night Sir Thomas.
Whither so late?
　　LOVELL
　　　　Came you from the King, my lord?
GARDINER
I did, Sir Thomas, and left him at primero

With the Duke of Suffolk.
   LOVELL
                  I must to him too
Before he go to bed. I'll take my leave.
   GARDINER
Not yet Sir Thomas Lovell. What's the matter?
It seems you are in haste; an if there be
No great offence belongs to't, give your friend
Some touch of your late business. Affairs that walk,
As they say spirits do, at midnight, have
In them a wilder nature than the business
That seeks dispatch by day.
   LOVELL
                  My lord, I love you;
And durst commend a secret to your ear
Much weightier than this work. The Queen's in labour,
They say in great extremity, and feared
She'll with the labour end.
   GARDINER
                  The fruit she goes with
I pray for heartily, that it may find
Good time, and live; but for the stock Sir Thomas,
I wish it grubbed up now.
   LOVELL
                  Methinks I could
Cry the amen, and yet my conscience says

Act five Scene one

She's a good creature, and, sweet lady, does
Deserve our better wishes.

GARDINER

                    But, sir, sir,
Hear me Sir Thomas, y'are a gentleman
Of mine own way. I know you wise, religious;
And let me tell you, it will ne'er be well,
'Twill not Sir Thomas Lovell, take't of me,
Till Cranmer, Cromwell, her two hands, and she,
Sleep in their graves.

LOVELL

                   Now sir, you speak of two
The most remarked i' th' kingdom. As for Cromwell,
Beside that of the Jewel House, is made Master
O' th' Rolls, and the King's Secretary; further sir,
Stands in the gap and trade of moe preferments,
With which the time will load him. Th' archbishop
Is the King's hand, and tongue, and who dare speak
One syllable against him?

GARDINER

                     Yes, yes, Sir Thomas,
There are that dare, and I myself have ventured
To speak my mind of him; and indeed this day,
Sir—I may tell it you—I think I have
Incensed the lords o' th' Council that he is—

For so I know he is, they know he is—
A most arch heretic, a pestilence
That does infect the land; with which they moved,
Have broken with the King, who hath so far
Given ear to our complaint, of his great grace
And princely care, foreseeing those fell mischiefs
Our reasons laid before him, hath commanded
To-morrow morning to the Council board
He be convented. He's a rank weed Sir Thomas,
And we must root him out. From your affairs
I hinder you too long. Good night, Sir Thomas.
   LOVELL
Many good nights, my lord. I rest your servant.
            [*Exeunt Gardiner and Page.*
Enter Henry and Suffolk.
   HENRY
Charles, I will play no more to-night,
My mind's not on't; you are too hard for me.
   SUFFOLK
Sir, I did never win of you before.
   HENRY
But little, Charles,
Nor shall not, when my fancy's on my play.
Now Lovell, from the Queen what is the news?
   LOVELL
            I could not personally deliver to her
What you commanded me, but by her woman
I sent your message, who returned her thanks

Act five Scene one

In the great'st humbleness, and desired your Highness
Most heartily to pray for her.
    HENRY
                         What sayst thou? Ha?
To pray for her? What, is she crying out?
    LOVELL
So said her woman, and that her suff'rance made
Almost each pang a death.
    HENRY
                      Alas good lady!
    SUFFOLK
God safely quit her of her burthen, and
With gentle travail, to the gladding of
Your Highness with an heir.
    HENRY
                    'Tis midnight Charles;
Prithee to bed, and in thy prayers remember
The estate of my poor Queen. Leave me alone,
For I must think of that which company
Would not be friendly to.
    SUFFOLK
                    I wish your Highness
A quiet night, and my good mistress will
Remember in my prayers.
    HENRY
        Charles, good night. [*Exit Suffolk.*
Enter Denny.
Well sir, what follows?

DENNY
Sir, I have brought my lord the archbishop 80
As you commanded me.
HENRY
                    Ha? Canterbury?
DENNY
Ay my good lord.
HENRY
                'Tis true. Where is he Denny?
DENNY
He attends your Highness' pleasure.
HENRY
                    Bring him to us. [*Exit Denny.*
LOVELL [*aside*]
This is about that which the bishop spake,
I am happily come hither. 85
Enter Cranmer and Denny.
HENRY
Avoid the gallery. [*Lovell delays going.*] Ha! I have said. Be gone.
What?   [*Exeunt Lovell and Denny.*
CRANMER [*aside*]
   I am fearful. Wherefore frowns he thus?
'Tis his aspect of terror. All's not well.
HENRY
How now my lord? You do desire to know
Wherefore I sent for you.
CRANMER [*kneels*]
                    It is my duty 90
T' attend your Highness' pleasure.

Act five Scene one   165
>HENRY
                          Pray you arise
My good and gracious Lord of Canterbury.
Come, you and I must walk a turn together,
I have news to tell you. Come, come, give me
   your hand.
Ah my good lord, I grieve at what I speak,   95
And am right sorry to repeat what follows.
I have, and most unwillingly, of late
Heard many grievous, I do say my lord
Grievous complaints of you; which being
   considered,
Have moved us, and our Council, that you shall   100
This morning come before us, where I know
You cannot with such freedom purge yourself,
But that till further trial in those charges
Which will require your answer, you must take
Your patience to you, and be well contented   105
To make your house our Tower; you a brother
   of us,
It fits we thus proceed, or else no witness
Would come against you.
>CRANMER [*kneels*]
                I humbly thank your Highness,
And am right glad to catch this good occasion
Most thoroughly to be winnowed, where my
   chaff   110
And corn shall fly asunder; for I know
There's none stands under more calumnious
   tongues,

Than I myself, poor man.
>   HENRY
>
>   Stand up, good Canterbury,
> Thy truth and thy integrity is rooted
> In us thy friend. Give me thy hand, stand up,
> Prithee let's walk. Now by my holidame,
> What manner of man are you! My lord, I looked
> You would have given me your petition, that
> I should have ta'en some pains to bring together
> Yourself and your accusers, and to have heard you
> Without indurance further.
>   CRANMER
>
>   Most dread liege,
> The good I stand on is my truth and honesty.
> If they shall fail, I with mine enemies
> Will triumph o'er my person, which I weigh not,
> Being of those virtues vacant. I fear nothing
> What can be said against me.
>   HENRY
>
>   Know you not
> How your state stands i' th' world, with the whole world?
> Your enemies are many, and not small; their practices
> Must bear the same proportion, and not ever
> The justice and the truth o' th' question carries
> The due o' th' verdict with it. At what ease
> Might corrupt minds procure knaves as corrupt

Act five Scene one

To swear against you; such things have been done.
You are potently opposed, and with a malice
Of as great size. Ween you of better luck, *135*
I mean in perjured witness, than your Master,
Whose minister you are, whiles here he lived
Upon this naughty earth? Go to, go to,
You take a precipice for no leap of danger,
And woo your own destruction.

CRANMER

                       God and your Majesty *140*
Protect mine innocence, or I fall into
The trap is laid for me.

HENRY

                       Be of good cheer.
They shall no more prevail than we give way to.
Keep comfort to you, and this morning see
You do appear before them. If they shall chance, *145*
In charging you with matters, to commit you,
The best persuasions to the contrary
Fail not to use, and with what vehemency
The occasion shall instruct you. If entreaties
Will render you no remedy, this ring *150*
Deliver them, and your appeal to us
There make before them. Look, the good man weeps:
He's honest on mine honour. God's blessed Mother,
I swear he is true-hearted, and a soul

None better in my kingdom. Get you gone,
And do as I have bid you. [*Exit Cranmer.*] He has strangled
His language in his tears.
    Enter Old Lady.
    GENTLEMAN [*within*]
Come back. What mean you?
    OLD LADY
I'll not come back; the tidings that I bring
Will make my boldness manners. Now good angels
Fly o'er thy royal head, and shade thy person
Under their blessed wings.
    HENRY
                Now by thy looks
I guess thy message. Is the Queen delivered?
Say ay, and of a boy.
    OLD LADY
                Ay, ay my liege,
And of a lovely boy. The God of heaven
Both now and ever bless her. 'Tis a girl
Promises boys hereafter. Sir, your Queen
Desires your visitation, and to be
Acquainted with this stranger; 'tis as like you,
As cherry is to cherry.
    HENRY
                Lovell.
    Enter Lovell.
    LOVELL
                Sir.

Act five Scene one 169

HENRY
Give her an hundred marks. I'll to the Queen. 170
[*Exit.*

OLD LADY
An hundred marks? By this light, I'll ha' more.
An ordinary groom is for such payment.
I will have more, or scold it out of him.
Said I for this, the girl was like to him?
I'll have more, or else unsay't; and now, 175
While 'tis hot, I'll put it to the issue. [*Exeunt.*

Scene two

Before the Council chamber.

Enter Pursuivants and others; then enter Cranmer.

CRANMER
I hope I am not too late, and yet the gentleman
That was sent to me from the Council prayed me
To make great haste. All fast? What means this? Ho!
Who waits there?
    Enter Doorkeeper.
          Sure you know me?
DOORKEEPER
                    Yes, my lord;
But yet I cannot help you. 5

CRANMER

Why?

DOORKEEPER

Your Grace must wait till you be called for.
Enter Butts.

CRANMER

So.

BUTTS [*aside*]

This is a piece of malice. I am glad
I came this way so happily. The King
Shall understand it presently.   [*Exit.*

CRANMER [*aside*]

'Tis Butts,   10
The King's physician; as he passed along,
How earnestly he cast his eyes upon me!
Pray heaven he sound not my disgrace. For certain,
This is of purpose laid by some that hate me—
God turn their hearts; I never sought their malice—   15
To quench mine honour. They would shame to make me
Wait else at door, a fellow councillor,
'Mong boys, grooms, and lackeys. But their pleasures
Must be fulfilled, and I attend with patience.
Enter Henry and Butts above.

BUTTS

I'll show your Grace the strangest sight—

Act five Scene two

HENRY
What's that Butts?
BUTTS
I think your Highness saw this many a day.
HENRY
Body a me, where is it?
BUTTS
There my lord:
The high promotion of his Grace of Canterbury,
Who holds his state at door, 'mongst pursuivants,
Pages, and footboys.
HENRY
Ha? 'Tis he indeed.
Is this the honour they do one another?
'Tis well there's one above 'em yet; I had thought
They had parted so much honesty among 'em,
At least good manners, as not thus to suffer
A man of his place, and so near our favour,
To dance attendance on their lordships' pleasures,
And at the door too, like a post with packets.
By holy Mary, Butts, there's knavery:
Let 'em alone, and draw the curtain close.
We shall hear more anon.

Scene three

The Council chamber.

A Council table brought in with chairs

and stools, and placed under the state. Enter Lord Chancellor, places himself at the upper end of the table, on the left hand; a seat being left void above him, as for Canterbury's seat; Suffolk, Norfolk, Surrey, Lord Chamberlain, Gardiner, seat themselves in order on each side. Cromwell at lower end, as Secretary.

LORD CHANCELLOR
Speak to the business, Master Secretary;
Why are we met in council?
　　CROMWELL
　　　　　　　　　　Please your honours,
The chief cause concerns his Grace of
　Canterbury.
　　GARDINER
Has he had knowledge of it?
　　CROMWELL
　　　　　　　　Yes.
　　NORFOLK
　　　　　　　　　　Who waits there?　5
　　DOORKEEPER
Without, my noble lords?
　　GARDINER
　　　　　　　　Yes.
　　DOORKEEPER
　　　　　　　　　My Lord Archbishop;

Act five Scene three   173

And has done half an hour, to know your
    pleasures.
        LORD CHANCELLOR
Let him come in.
        DOORKEEPER
            Your Grace may enter now.
    [*Cranmer approaches the Council table.*
        LORD CHANCELLOR
My good Lord Archbishop, I'm very sorry
To sit here at this present, and behold
That chair stand empty. But we all are men   10
In our own natures frail and capable
Of our flesh; few are angels; out of which frailty
And want of wisdom, you that best should teach
    us,
Have misdemeaned yourself, and not a little,
Toward the King first, then his laws, in filling   15
The whole realm, by your teaching and your
    chaplains—
For so we are informed—with new opinions,
Divers and dangerous; which are heresies;
And not reformed, may prove pernicious.
        GARDINER
Which reformation must be sudden too   20
My noble lords; for those that tame wild horses
Pace 'em not in their hands to make 'em gentle;
But stop their mouths with stubborn bits and
    spur 'em,
Till they obey the manage. If we suffer,

Out of our easiness and childish pity
To one man's honour, this contagious sickness,
Farewell all physic; and what follows then?
Commotions, uproars, with a general taint
Of the whole state, as of late days our neighbours,
The upper Germany, can dearly witness,
Yet freshly pitied in our memories.

CRANMER

My good lords—hitherto, in all the progress
Both of my life and office, I have laboured,
And with no little study, that my teaching,
And the strong course of my authority,
Might go one way, and safely; and the end
Was ever to do well: nor is there living—
I speak it with a single heart, my lords—
A man that more detests, more stirs against,
Both in his private conscience, and his place,
Defacers of a public peace than I do.
Pray heaven the King may never find a heart
With less allegiance in it. Men that make
Envy and crooked malice nourishment
Dare bite the best. I do beseech your lordships,
That in this case of justice my accusers,
Be what they will, may stand forth face to face,
And freely urge against me.

SUFFOLK

                Nay, my lord,
That cannot be; you are a councillor,
And by that virtue no man dare accuse you.

Act five Scene three

GARDINER
My lord, because we have business of more moment,
We will be short with you. 'Tis his Highness' pleasure,
And our consent, for better trial of you,
From hence you be committed to the Tower;
Where being but a private man again, 55
You shall know many dare accuse you boldly,
More than, I fear, you are provided for.

CRANMER
Ah my good Lord of Winchester—I thank you,
You are always my good friend; if your will pass,
I shall both find your lordship judge and juror, 60
You are so merciful. I see your end,
'Tis my undoing. Love and meekness, lord,
Become a churchman better than ambition;
Win straying souls with modesty again,
Cast none away. That I shall clear myself, 65
Lay all the weight ye can upon my patience,
I make as little doubt as you do conscience
In doing daily wrongs. I could say more,
But reverence to your calling makes me modest.

GARDINER
My lord, my lord, you are a sectary, 70
That's the plain truth; your painted gloss discovers,
To men that understand you, words and weakness.

CROMWELL
My Lord of Winchester, you are a little,
By your good favour, too sharp; men so noble,
However faulty, yet should find respect
For what they have been: 'tis a cruelty
To load a falling man.
GARDINER
                    Good Master Secretary,
I cry your honour mercy; you may worst
Of all this table say so.
CROMWELL
                    Why my lord?
GARDINER
Do not I know you for a favourer
Of this new sect? Ye are not sound.
CROMWELL
                              Not sound?
GARDINER
Not sound I say.
CROMWELL
              Would you were half so honest.
Men's prayers then would seek you, not their fears.
GARDINER
I shall remember this bold language.
CROMWELL
                              Do.
Remember your bold life too.
LORD CHANCELLOR
                    This is too much;

Act five Scene three

Forbear for shame my lords.
>GARDINER
>>I have done.
>CROMWELL
>>And I.
>LORD CHANCELLOR

Then thus for you, my lord, it stands agreed
I take it, by all voices, that forthwith
You be conveyed to th' Tower a prisoner;
There to remain till the King's further pleasure 90
Be known unto us. Are you all agreed lords?
>ALL

We are.
>CRANMER
>>Is there no other way of mercy,

But I must needs to th' Tower, my lords?
>GARDINER
>>What other

Would you expect? You are strangely troublesome.
Let some o' th' guard be ready there.
>*Enter Guard.*
>CRANMER
>>For me? 95

Must I go like a traitor thither?
>GARDINER
>>Receive him,

And see him safe i' th' Tower.
>CRANMER
>>Stay, good my lords,

I have a little yet to say. Look there my lords,
By virtue of that ring I take my cause
Out of the gripes of cruel men, and give it 100
To a most noble judge, the King my master.
    LORD CHAMBERLAIN
This is the King's ring.
    SURREY
                    'Tis no counterfeit.
    SUFFOLK
'Tis the right ring, by heaven. I told ye all,
When we first put this dangerous stone a-rolling,
'Twould fall upon ourselves.
    NORFOLK
                    Do you think my lords, 105
The King will suffer but the little finger
Of this man to be vexed?
    LORD CHAMBERLAIN
                    'Tis now too certain.
How much more is his life in value with him!
Would I were fairly out on't. [*Exit Henry above.*
    CROMWELL
                    My mind gave me,
In seeking tales and informations 110
Against this man, whose honesty the devil
And his disciples only envy at,
Ye blew the fire that burns ye—

    Enter Henry below.

                    now have at ye!
                    [*Henry takes his seat.*

Act five Scene three

GARDINER

Dread sovereign, how much are we bound to heaven,
In daily thanks, that gave us such a Prince;
Not only good and wise, but most religious:
One that in all obedience makes the Church
The chief aim of his honour, and to strengthen
That holy duty, out of dear respect,
His royal self in judgement comes to hear
The cause betwixt her and this great offender.

HENRY

You were ever good at sudden commendations,
Bishop of Winchester. But know I come not
To hear such flattery now, and in my presence
They are too thin and base to hide offences.
To me you cannot reach you play the spaniel,
And think with wagging of your tongue to win me.
But whatsoe'er thou tak'st me for, I'm sure
Thou hast a cruel nature and a bloody.
[*To Cranmer.*] Good man, sit down. Now let me see the proudest
He, that dares most, but wag his finger at thee.
By all that's holy, he had better starve,
Than but once think his place becomes thee not.

SURREY

May it please your Grace—

HENRY

No sir, it does not please me.

I had thought I had had men of some understanding
And wisdom of my Council; but I find none.
Was it discretion lords, to let this man,
This good man—few of you deserve that title—
This honest man, wait like a lousy footboy
At chamber door? And one as great as you are?
Why, what a shame was this! Did my commission
Bid ye so far forget yourselves? I gave ye
Power, as he was a councillor to try him,
Not as a groom. There's some of ye, I see,
More out of malice than integrity,
Would try him to the utmost, had ye mean,
Which ye shall never have while I live.

LORD CHANCELLOR

Thus far
My most dread sovereign, may it like your Grace,
To let my tongue excuse all. What was purposed
Concerning his imprisonment, was rather,
If there be faith in men, meant for his trial,
And fair purgation to the world, than malice,
I'm sure in me.

HENRY

Well, well, my lords, respect him,
Take him, and use him well; he's worthy of it.
I will say thus much for him, if a Prince
May be beholding to a subject, I
Am for his love and service so to him.
Make me no more ado, but all embrace him;

Act five Scene three

Be friends for shame my lords. My Lord of Canterbury,
I have a suit which you must not deny me.
That is, a fair young maid that yet wants baptism,
You must be godfather, and answer for her.
 CRANMER
The greatest monarch now alive may glory
In such an honour; how may I deserve it,
That am a poor and humble subject to you?
 HENRY
Come come, my lord, you'd spare your spoons.
You shall have two noble partners with you; the old Duchess of Norfolk, and Lady Marquess Dorset. Will these please you?
Once more my Lord of Winchester, I charge you
Embrace and love this man.
 GARDINER
      With a true heart
And brother-love I do it.
 CRANMER
      And let heaven
Witness, how dear I hold this confirmation.
 HENRY
Good man, those joyful tears show thy true heart.
The common voice I see is verified
Of thee, which says thus, do my Lord of Canterbury
A shrewd turn, and he's your friend for ever.
Come lords, we trifle time away; I long

To have this young one made a Christian.
As I have made ye one, lords, one remain;
So I grow stronger, you more honour gain.
                              [*Exeunt.*

Scene four

Before the palace.

Noise and tumult within. Enter Porter and Man.

PORTER
You'll leave your noise anon, ye rascals. Do you take the Court for Parish Garden? Ye rude slaves, leave your gaping.

VOICE [*within*]
Good master porter I belong to th' larder.

PORTER
Belong to th' gallows, and be hanged, ye rogue! Is this a place to roar in? Fetch me a dozen crab-tree staves, and strong ones; these are but switches to 'em. I'll scratch your heads; you must be seeing christenings? Do you look for ale and cakes here, you rude rascals?

MAN
Pray sir be patient; 'tis as much impossible,
Unless we sweep 'em from the door with
    cannons,
To scatter 'em, as 'tis to make 'em sleep
On May-day morning, which will never be.

We may as well push against Powle's as stir 'em.
PORTER
How got they in, and be hanged?
MAN
Alas I know not, how gets the tide in?
As much as one sound cudgel of four foot—
You see the poor remainder—could distribute,   20
I made no spare sir.
PORTER
               You did nothing sir.
MAN
I am not Samson, nor Sir Guy, nor Colebrand,
To mow 'em down before me; but if I spared any
That had a head to hit, either young or old,
He or she, cuckold or cuckold-maker,   25
Let me ne'er hope to see a chine again,
And that I would not for a cow, God save her.
VOICE [*within*]
Do you hear master porter?
PORTER
I shall be with you presently, good master puppy.
Keep the door close sirrah.   30
MAN
What would you have me do?
PORTER
What should you do, but knock 'em down by th' dozens? Is this Moorfields to muster in? Or have we some strange Indian with the great tool come to Court, the women so besiege us? Bless me,   35
what a fry of fornication is at door! On my

Christian conscience this one christening will beget a thousand; here will be father, godfather, and all together.

MAN

The spoons will be the bigger sir. There is a fellow somewhat near the door, he should be a brazier by his face, for o' my conscience twenty of the dog-days now reign in's nose; all that stand about him are under the line, they need no other penance. That fire-drake did I hit three times on the head, and three times was his nose discharged against me; he stands there like a mortar-piece to blow us. There was a haberdasher's wife of small wit, near him, that railed upon me, till her pinked porringer fell off her head, for kindling such a combustion in the state. I missed the meteor once, and hit that woman, who cried out, clubs, when I might see from far some forty truncheoners draw to her succour, which were the hope o' th' Strond where she was quartered; they fell on, I made good my place; at length they came to th' broomstaff to me, I defied 'em still, when suddenly a file of boys behind 'em, loose shot, delivered such a shower of pebbles, that I was fain to draw mine honour in, and let 'em win the work: the devil was amongst 'em I think surely.

PORTER

These are the youths that thunder at a playhouse, and fight for bitten apples, that no audience but

Act five Scene four

the tribulation of Tower Hill, or the limbs of
Limehouse, their dear brothers, are able to endure. I have some of 'em in Limbo Patrum, and
there they are like to dance these three days;
besides the running banquet of two beadles that
is to come.

Enter Lord Chamberlain

LORD CHAMBERLAIN
Mercy o' me, what a multitude are here!
They grow still too; from all parts they are coming,
As if we kept a fair here. Where are these porters,
These lazy knaves? Y'have made a fine hand fellows.
There's a trim rabble let in; are all these
Your faithful friends o' th' suburbs? We shall have
Great store of room no doubt left for the ladies,
When they pass back from the christening.

PORTER
      An't please your honour,
We are but men; and what so many may do,
Not being torn apieces, we have done
An army cannot rule 'em.

LORD CHAMBERLAIN
      As I live,
If the King blame me for't, I'll lay ye all
By th' heels, and suddenly; and on your heads
Clap round fines for neglect. Y'are lazy knaves,

And here ye lie baiting of bombards, when
Ye should do service. Hark the trumpets sound;
Th'are come already from the christening.
Go break among the press, and find a way out
To let the troop pass fairly; or I'll find
A Marshalsea shall hold ye play these two
  months.
    PORTER
Make way there for the Princess.
    MAN
You great fellow, stand close up, or I'll make
your head ache.
    PORTER
You i' th' chamblet, get up o' th' rail, I'll
peck you o'er the pales else.

Scene five

> *The same.*
>
> *Enter trumpets sounding: then two Aldermen, Lord Mayor, Garter, Cranmer, Duke of Norfolk with his Marshall's staff, Duke of Suffolk, two Noblemen, bearing great standing-bowls for the christening gifts: then four Noblemen bearing a canopy, under which the Duchess of Norfolk, godmother, bearing the child richly habited in a mantle, etc., train borne by a Lady: then follows the*

Act five Scene five

Marchioness Dorset, the other godmother, and Ladies. The troop pass once about the stage, and Garter speaks.

GARTER
Heaven from thy endless goodness, send prosperous life, long and ever happy, to the high and mighty Princess of England, Elizabeth.
Flourish. Enter Henry and Guard.
CRANMER [*kneels*]
And to your royal Grace, and the good Queen, 5
My noble partners and myself thus pray
All comfort, joy in this most gracious lady
Heaven ever laid up to make parents happy,
May hourly fall upon ye.
HENRY
       Thank you good Lord Archbishop.
What is her name?
CRANMER
      Elizabeth.
HENRY
           Stand up lord. 10
[*Henry kisses the child.*
With this kiss take my blessing. God protect thee,
Into whose hand I give thy life.
CRANMER
       Amen.
HENRY
My noble gossips, y'have been too prodigal;

I thank ye heartily. So shall this lady,
When she has so much English.
CRANMER
Let me speak sir,
For heaven now bids me; and the words I utter
Let none think flattery, for they'll find 'em truth.
This royal infant—heaven still move about her—
Though in her cradle, yet now promises
Upon this land a thousand thousand blessings,
Which time shall bring to ripeness. She shall be—
But few now living can behold that goodness—
A pattern to all princes living with her,
And all that shall succeed. Saba was never
More covetous of wisdom and fair virtue
Than this pure soul shall be. All princely graces
That mould up such a mighty piece as this is,
With all the virtues that attend the good,
Shall still be doubled on her. Truth shall nurse her,
Holy and heavenly thoughts still counsel her.
She shall be loved and feared. Her own shall bless her;
Her foes shake like a field of beaten corn,
And hang their heads with sorrow. Good grows with her.
In her days, every man shall eat in safety
Under his own vine what he plants; and sing
The merry songs of peace to all his neighbours.
God shall be truly known, and those about her

Act five Scene five

From her shall read the perfect ways of honour,
And by those claim their greatness, not by blood.
Nor shall this peace sleep with her; but as when
The bird of wonder dies, the maiden phoenix,
Her ashes new create another heir,
As great in admiration as herself,
So shall she leave her blessedness to one,
When heaven shall call her from this cloud of darkness,
Who from the sacred ashes of her honour
Shall star-like rise, as great in fame as she was,
And so stand fixed. Peace, plenty, love, truth, terror,
That were the servants to this chosen infant,
Shall then be his, and like a vine grow to him.
Wherever the bright sun of heaven shall shine,
His honour, and the greatness of his name,
Shall be, and make new nations. He shall flourish,
And like a mountain cedar reach his branches
To all the plains about him. Our children's children
Shall see this, and bless heaven.

HENRY
                    Thou speakest wonders.

CRANMER
She shall be, to the happiness of England,
An aged Princess; many days shall see her,
And yet no day without a deed to crown it.
Would I had known no more, but she must die—

She must, the saints must have her—yet a virgin,
A most unspotted lily, shall she pass
To th' ground, and all the world shall mourn her.

HENRY
O Lord Archbishop,
Thou hast made me now a man; never before
This happy child did I get any thing.
This oracle of comfort has so pleased me,
That when I am in heaven I shall desire
To see what this child does, and praise my Maker.
I thank ye all. To you my good Lord Mayor,
And your good brethren, I am much beholding;
I have received much honour by your presence,
And ye shall find me thankful. Lead the way lords,
Ye must all see the Queen, and she must thank ye;
She will be sick else. This day, no man think
Has business at his house; for all shall stay.
This little one shall make it holiday. [*Exeunt.*

Epilogue

'Tis ten to one, this play can never please
All that are here. Some come to take their ease,
And sleep an act or two; but those, we fear,
W'have frighted with our trumpets; so 'tis clear,

Epilogue

They'll say 'tis naught. Others to hear the city
Abused extremely, and to cry, that's witty,
Which we have not done neither; that I fear
All the expected good w'are like to hear,
For this play at this time, is only in
The merciful construction of good women,
For such a one we showed 'em. If they smile,
And say 'twill do, I know within a while
All the best men are ours; for 'tis ill hap,
If they hold when their ladies bid 'em clap.

Shakespeare and His Theatre

BY FRANCIS FERGUSSON

I. SHAKESPEARE'S CAREER

William Shakespeare was christened in Stratford on April twenty-sixth, 1564. The exact date of his birth is unknown, but it is traditionally celebrated on the twenty-third, because that is Saint George's Day, and Saint George is England's patron saint.

The Shakespeares were a prosperous and locally prominent family. William was the oldest of six children. His father, John Shakespeare, the son of a tenant farmer, had moved to Stratford as a young man, and there built for himself a successful business career as a glover and a dealer in wool, timber, and other commodities. John also held office as Justice of the Peace and High Bailiff (Mayor); and late in life he was granted a coat of arms, which made him a "gentleman." Shakespeare's mother, Mary Arden, a member of a family of small landowners, must have brought her husband both social standing and land.

Stratford, about a hundred miles northwest of London, was a prosperous market town, one of the largest in Warwickshire. A great deal is known about Stratford, which enables us to understand something of Shakespeare's boyhood there. The town supported a grammar school which was free to the sons of Burgesses, of whom Shakespeare was one. Grammar schools were designed to prepare their students for one of the universities, and in Stratford the masters were university graduates. The education they gave was narrow but thorough. It included some history and religious instruction, but was based chiefly on Latin and the arts of language: grammar, logic, rhetoric, and what we call "public speaking." Shakespeare read a number of Latin authors, including Ovid and probably Plautus, whose comedies he imitated when he started to write for the stage. The children went to school on weekdays, summer and winter, from seven in the morning until five in the afternoon, with two hours off for dinner. Shakespeare must have started this strict routine as soon as he knew his catechism.

During his boyhood Stratford was regularly visited by touring players, including the best companies in England. The plays they brought were moralizing works on Biblical or classical themes, very wooden compared with what Shakespeare himself would write. But his future profession was highly esteemed; the players were received in the Guildhall by leading citizens, including no doubt Shakespeare's father. For the rest, we may safely imagine Shakespeare as engaged in the usual activities of a boy in a country town, acquiring the intimate knowledge of the countryside and its rural types which is reflected in his plays.

We do not know what Shakespeare did between the time he left school and his departure for London. Some of the stories about him—that he was for a time a country schoolmaster, that he got into trouble for poaching deer—are possible, but unproved. We do know that he married Ann Hathaway, daughter of a yeoman farmer, in 1582, when he was eighteen and she was twenty-three. Their first child, Susan, was baptized six months later. Perhaps the Shakespeares were "betrothed"—which, by the custom of the time, would have made them legally married—some months before the recorded church ceremony. They had two more children, the twins Hamnet, and Judith, who were christened in 1585. Shakespeare departed for London very soon after that. He did not take his family with him, for he occupied bachelor's lodgings in London for most of the rest of his life. But he was also a householder in Stratford, and apparently continued to think of himself as a resident.

London, when Shakespeare went there as a young man, in about 1586, was enjoying the great years of Queen Elizabeth's reign. She had ascended the throne in 1558; in 1588 her navy had its famous victory over the Spanish Armada, which marked England's emergence as a great sea-power, and symbolized the national rebirth. The City of London had its ancient mercantile traditions, its bourgeois freedoms, and, among the City officials, a certain Puritanical spirit of its own. But the City had spread far beyond the medieval walls, and Renaissance London contained between 100,000 and 200,000 inhabitants. As the seat of Elizabeth's court it was the unrivaled center of English politics and culture. It was a university town, for the Inns of Court, resident law-schools for young gentlemen of wealth, were there; and it was full of foreigners from the continent of Europe. As a great port it was in touch with the Indies, the Mediterranean, and the Americas. Shakespeare never went to a university, but London was admirably fitted to complete his education in Italian and French, in history and literature, in the great professions, and to give him direct experience of the ways of men at an exciting moment in history. The theatre was near the center of life in Renaissance London, and Shakespeare must have been close to many of the great figures and great events of his time.

Much is known about London and about the theatres where Shakespeare worked, but little is known directly about his own doings. Contemporary comments on him, and on his plays, suggest that most of his great vitality went straight into his work for the theatre. Legal and business documents, church records, and the like, enable the experts to fix a few important dates in his personal and professional life. And the dates of his plays, though disputed in detail, are well enough established to give us the approximate sequence. It is chiefly through a study of his plays in the order in which he wrote them, and in relation to the known facts of his life, that we can gain some understanding of his development. It is convenient (following Professor Peter Alexander and others) to distinguish four main periods in Shakespeare's career:

I. Apprenticeship to the London Theatre: From Shakespeare's arrival in London (circa 1586) until he joined The Lord Chamberlain's Men, in 1594.

Shakespeare entered the theatre as an actor when he first

went to London, or as soon thereafter as he had acquired the necessary training. He was to be an actor and actor-manager for the rest of his life, and in that capacity, rather than as a playwright, he made a very good living. Playwrights received a smaller share of the theatre's revenue then than they do now. They sold their scripts outright, for very small sums, to the actors, who then divided the receipts among themselves. Shakespeare, however, began to write at once. By 1594 he had completed the following list: *Titus Andronicus; Henry VI*, Parts 1, 2, and 3; *The Comedy of Errors; Two Gentlemen of Verona; The Taming of the Shrew; Richard III; Love's Labor's Lost;* and probably *King John.*

Shakespeare's earliest work shows that he began his professional career in the most natural way: by mastering several kinds of plays that were then popular. *The Comedy of Errors, Two Gentlemen of Verona,* and *The Taming of the Shrew* are farces, based on the Latin comedy of Plautus. They have little of the poetry and subtlety of his later and more original comedies, but they are still, as they were when he wrote them, sure and effective popular entertainment. *Titus Andronicus*, a "Senecan" melodrama like other pseudo-classical plays of the time, was successful then, but usually proves too sensational and pompous for the modern stage.

The three parts of *Henry VI* are the first of Shakespeare's "Histories." The history play was a popular and characteristic form in the London theatre as Shakespeare found it. It was taken from one of the widely read Chronicles of English history, like those of Shakespeare's favorite Holinshed—a dramatization of some exciting sequence from the epic struggle of the Crown against the great nobles, the intriguing churchmen, and France and Spain. Shakespeare's generation felt that this struggle had been victoriously concluded with Elizabeth. The history plays express a somewhat jingoistic nationalism, but also, in Shakespeare's plays at least, the passion for social order and the cautious political wisdom which were making England great. *Henry VI* is the crudest of Shakespeare's Histories; it gallops, with the speed of a boy's adventure story, from one high-pitched quarrel to the next. Yet one can find in it the beginnings of some of his great and lifelong themes.

The next Histories, *Richard III* and *King John,* and the comedy, *Love's Labor's Lost,* hardly belong to Shakespeare's apprenticeship. *Love's Labor's Lost* is particularly interesting: it was written, apparently, for the Court instead of the popular audience of the public theatres. It is a gently ironic picture of an aristocratic circle infatuated with neoplatonic notions of love and learning; and it shows that Shakespeare was already at home in the "best society," and in the fashionable literary humanism of the Renaissance.

As though all this were not enough, the young Shakespeare spent part of the years 1592-94, when the Plague made one of its descents upon London and the theatres were closed, writing his narrative poems, *Venus and Adonis, The Rape of Lucrece,* and *The Phoenix and the Turtle,* and perhaps some of the sonnets too. He dedicated *Venus and Adonis* to Southhampton, the famous patron of the arts. It was immediately successful, and it made Shakespeare's reputation as a writer in circles where the theatre was not considered polite literature.

I have called this period "apprenticeship," but Shakespeare began to find himself almost at once. He was born with his genius for theatrical story-telling, and also that easy sympathy with men and ideas which enabled him to share the life of his times at every point. He had, above all, the ability to learn from his own playwriting experience. Before 1594 he was already rethinking his discoveries, thereby swiftly deepening both his vision and his art.

II. Growing Mastery: From 1594, when Shakespeare joined The Lord Chamberlain's Men, to 1599, when the Globe Theatre opened.

The Lord Chamberlain's Men, which Shakespeare joined in 1594, was the company of actor-managers with whom he was to work for the rest of his life. It was the best company in London, including Richard Burbage, soon to be recognized as England's leading actor; Heminge and Condell, who were to publish the First Folio of Shakespeare's plays after his death; and Will Kempe, the renowned comedian. Their patron, the Lord Chamberlain (Lord Hunsdon) was a member of the Queen's Privy Council, in charge of her household and all the entertainments. He did not support his players; their income came mostly from their large public audiences. But he lent them the prestige of the Crown, defended them from the officials of the City of London (who had a bourgeois and puritanical mistrust of the theatre), and arranged for their frequent and well-paid appearances at Court. In addition to regular performances in the public theatres and at Court, The Lord Chamberlain's Men toured the provinces in the summer, and sometimes at other seasons also, when the Plague forced the closing of the City theatres.

In 1595 Shakespeare's only son, Hamnet, died in Stratford at the age of eleven. In 1597 he bought New Place, the largest house in Stratford, evidence that he was making a good living, and also that he continued to think of himself as a resident of his native town.

He wrote the following plays in approximately this period: *Romeo and Juliet; Richard II; Henry IV*, Parts 1 and 2; *The Merchant of Venice; A Midsummer Night's Dream; The Merry Wives of Windsor; Much Ado about Nothing; Henry V; As You Like It;* and perhaps *Twelfth Night*.

These are the plays of the most popular playwright of the day: Shakespeare was giving his public what it wanted. But he was also unfolding, through the popular tales he dramatized, his own intimate sense of human life. The plays may be classified as Comedies, Histories, and Tragedies, but each one is unique. They owe more to Shakespeare's own flexible art than they do to the theatrical conventions he inherited.

Richard II and *Henry IV*, Parts 1 and 2, are freer and deeper in language, in their rather disillusioned political wisdom, and above all in their character-drawing, than the early Histories. By the time he wrote *Henry V* Shakespeare seems to have tired of the History play, tied as it was to familiar events and to the immediate issues of politics. In the next phase he will turn from literal history to the freer and deeper form of tragedy.

The comedies of this period, the "Golden Comedies," are far more original in form and spirit than the "plotty" Latin farces of his apprenticeship. The titles and subtitles (*As You Like It*, or *Twelfth Night, Or What You Will*, for instance) suggest that Shakespeare was meeting a public demand for more plays like *A Midsummer Night's Dream*. But at the same time he was exploring an inspiration of his own. He had learned to combine several stories of different kinds in such a way as to suggest, in each play, a single poetic and ruefully smiling vision of human life. He presents the delusions of youth as fond and charming; he stages them in the light of dream, or of some brief festive occasion. The only exception is *The Merry Wives*, a farce which he may have written at the Queen's request.

The Merchant of Venice and *Romeo and Juliet* are akin in spirit to the comedies, but each represents also a new discovery. *The Merchant* is Shakespeare's first serious play about a commercial republic, and his first ambitious experiment in allegory. *Romeo and Juliet* brings into the theatre, for the first time, the themes, the music, and even the verse-forms of a very old tradition in European love-poetry, and in its structure foreshadows the great tragedies of the next phase.

In these intense five years Shakespeare's genius was coming into its own, and one can see its growth in every aspect of his complex art. His fabulous gift is most evident, perhaps, in the great characters that suddenly people his stage. Harry and Falstaff in *Henry IV*, Shylock in *The Merchant*, the Nurse in *Romeo*, Beatrice and Benedick in *Much Ado*, must have surprised even their author. One can see that Shakespeare's imagination was fed by the lively types that swarmed around him in London, and also by the actors whom he knew so well in his own company. A working theatre is a small society in itself, analogous to the larger human world around it. One can often feel, in the many-sided humanity of Shakespeare's characters—their fatness or leanness, their tricks of speech, life-rhythms that express certain temperaments—the presence of flesh-and-blood actors who would perform them. Perhaps Shakespeare's creations owe as much to his acting-company as to the stories he used. Yet in the long run they live with the life of Shakespeare's poetic imagination, which is more intense than any direct mimicry could be.

> *III. Maturity: The years of the great tragedies, from the acquisition of the Globe Theatre in 1599 to the acquisition of the Blackfriars' Theatre in 1608.*

In 1599 The Lord Chamberlain's Men acquired the illustrious Globe Theatre, which they were to occupy for the rest of Shakespeare's life. Elizabeth died in 1603, and James I ascended the throne. Fortunately James was as fond of the theatre as Elizabeth had been. He made The Lord Chamberlain's Men "The King's Men," thus taking Shakespeare's company under his royal patronage, and recognizing it as the finest in London. The King's Men seem to have enjoyed almost unbroken success, for they played often at Court and continued to attract large audiences at the Globe.

Shakespeare wrote the following plays in this period of eight or nine years: *Julius Caesar; Hamlet; All's Well That Ends Well; Troilus and Cressida; Measure for Measure; Othello; King Lear; Macbeth; Antony and Cleopatra; Timon of Athens; Coriolanus.*

The list looks to succeeding generations like a unique but natural miracle, a Sequoia Forest of the human spirit. No one has succeeded in mapping it satisfactorily, and every new reader is free to enjoy and explore it as his own understanding slowly grows.

Many attempts have been made to "explain" Shakespeare's tragic phase as the result of circumstances in his own life. We know that Hamnet, his only son, died in 1596, his father in 1601, and his mother in 1608. The last years of Queen Elizabeth's reign were darkened by trouble at home and abroad, especially her long quarrel with Essex. James's reign too, after a brief period of hopefulness, was filled with the beginnings of disorder. All over Europe the end of the Renaissance was a time of confusion and frightening premonitions of change. All of this, and probably more intimate experiences of which we know nothing, must have been grist to Shakespeare's mill. But the crucial question, how experience is transmuted into tragic poetry, is unanswerable.

The most illuminating studies are based on the plays themselves, and their relationships to earlier work, for Shakespeare (like other great artists) learned continually by rethinking his own achievements. It has been pointed out that some of the tragic characters grew, by mysterious processes of transformation and combination, out of their predecessors: Hamlet from Richard II, Brutus, Romeo; Macbeth from Richard III, perhaps Bolingbroke in *Richard II* and *Henry IV*. Shakespeare's mature mastery of versification, and also of form and plot, were the outcome of long practice; the musical harmony of imagery and symbol in a late play like *Antony and Cleopatra* was the fruit of years of writing. About the turn of the century the varied elements fell into place, and Shakespeare began to enjoy his full mastery.

The tragedies proper, especially *Hamlet, King Lear*, and *Macbeth*, which have to do with the tragic paradoxes of kingship, may be thought of as deeper mutations of the Histories. Like the Histories, these three plays picture the kind of society that Shakespeare knew and loved best, that of the Tudor monarchy. But Hamlet's Denmark, Lear's ancient Britain, and Macbeth's Scotland are not literally contemporary England. The stories of those plays are not, like the Histories, connected with familiar political struggles. Intimate as they are in detail, immediate though their life is—and instantly convincing—they have at the same time a certain legendary distance. They are mirrors in which Shakespeare could freely reflect the universal meanings he had found in his own and his country's experience.

The Roman tragedies, *Julius Caesar* and *Coriolanus*, are also derived from the Histories, but the Roman setting gives them a different quality. The characters and many details in these plays are Tudor English, but there is no doubt that Shakespeare wished them to evoke ancient Rome. Rome and its history had haunted the imagination of Europe since the dark ages, and Shakespeare's imagination since his schooldays; but he did not love Rome as he loved (and sometimes despaired of) his own monarchical society. He sees the fate of a Brutus or a Coriolanus in a colder and harder human world; between the mob one way and the wise but helpless philosophy of a Menenius, or the rationalizations of Brutus himself, the other way. In short, Rome, or the legendary idea of Rome, gave him another mirror in which to reflect another aspect of his tragic vision. And *Othello* reflects it in still another context. Set (like *The Merchant of Venice* and *Timon of Athens*) in a commercial republic, it is Shakespeare's most modern or "domestic" tragedy, foreshadowing Ibsen's well-made drama of individualism.

Even if one thinks only of the plays properly called "Tragedies," one can see that Shakespeare's sense of human destiny had not only deepened but widened, and now included most of the forms of human life and society visible at that time, the threshold of the modern world. But what are we to say of the other plays in the list? *Antony and Cleopatra*, for all its mortal sadness, hardly feels "tragic"; it floats like a dream, a transfiguration of the Golden Comedies. *Measure for Measure*, akin both to *Hamlet* and *The Tempest*, is a self-conscious political and theological allegory. *Troilus and Cressida*, conceived perhaps as a gigantic farce, has come to seem, since the early 'thirties, a prophetic picture of our own faithless "wars and lecheries." And so on. We cannot hope to grasp all of the aspects of Shakespeare's vision as it unfolded in these years, to say nothing of holding them all together.

But we can safely say that, just as the facts show that he was enjoying brilliant professional success, so the plays show "success" in a more intimate sense. The human creature must have appeared to him in an appalling light: "We that are young/ Shall never see so much, or live so long." But when we read the plays and hear their music, we are reminded that the tragic emotion includes exaltation. To have faced and then projected the tragic vision in poetry was a triumph of spirit. Shakespeare completed the great labors of his maturity in undiminished strength. Then he went on to digest the tragic vision in its turn, placing it in the serener perspective of the end of his life in the theatre.

IV. Synthesis and Serenity: From the acquisition of the Blackfriars' Theatre in 1608 to Shakespeare's death in Stratford in 1616.

The King's Men bought the Blackfriars' Theatre in 1608, and thereafter used it regularly, in bad weather, in addition to their Globe Theatre. Blackfriars' was so called because it was in one of the monasteries which had been taken over by the Crown under Henry VIII. It was an indoor theatre, and had been used for some years by a company of boy-actors. The influence of its indoor stage can be seen in Shakespeare's last plays; and the increasing use of indoor stages from this time onward prepared the evolution of the modern theatre. The "Inn-yard theatres," like the Globe, for which most of Shakespeare's plays were written, were soon to disappear.

The purchase of Blackfriars' is one of several signs that Shakespeare was ending his theatrical career in comfort and prosperity. Some time after 1610 he began, probably gradually, to retire from active work in the theatre, and his last days were spent in his house, New Place, in Stratford. His bequests, including the famous one of his "second-best bed" to his wife, reveal a very substantial citizen of his native town. His small legacies to fellow members of The King's Men show his respect and affection for his lifelong colleagues; and the preface which Heminge and Condell wrote for their First Folio of his plays shows that they continued to revere him eight years after his death. Shakespeare's company must have possessed some rare virtues in addition to their talent, for The King's Men lasted longer than any theatre group in the English-speaking world, before or since. And Shakespeare's art owes a great deal to the acting ensemble for which he wrote.

He completed the following plays in this period: *Pericles; Cymbeline; The Winter's Tale; The Tempest;* and *Henry VIII*.

Henry VIII completes Shakespeare's chronicle of English history with the auspicious birth of Elizabeth, but it is a pageant and an allegory, rather than a History like the earlier plays which are so called. It is more interesting to the modern reader for the indirect light it sheds on Shakespeare's politics than as a play in its own right.

The other four plays, which were written in the order in which they are listed above, represent the harmonious end of Shakespeare's career. They are not tragedies, but theatre-poetry with subtle and manifold allegorical meanings. Each of their stories covers a whole generation, from childhood to age, instead of a single profound crisis like the stories of the tragedies. They are full of echoes of the earlier themes, as though Shakespeare were looking back over the course of his life and art. *The Tempest* is the last, the richest, and the most assured masterpiece of the four. Miranda and Ferdinand give us again the music of youth and its brave new world; the usurping Duke, with his treacheries, reminds us of the themes of guilt and suffering in the Histories and Tragedies. All these figures—and Caliban and Ariel and Gonzago and the rest—are lovingly brooded over by the Magician, Prospero, now ready to renounce the glorious cares of art and rule. It is natural to see Prospero as an image of Shakespeare, and the play as his own last word on the form and meaning of his own career, a detached but moving reflection of life from the cradle to the grave. Such a reading confirms the impression one gets from the sequence of Shakespeare's plays, and from the known facts of his life: that, more than any other man, he knew and gratefully accepted the mysterious experience of everyman.

Shakespeare did not impress his contemporaries as a spectacular personality, though many of them knew he was the foremost dramatist of that, or perhaps any, age. Ben Jonson, in the verses he wrote to go with the portrait in the First Folio, speaks for all who attempt to picture Shakespeare:

To the Reader.

This Figure, that thou here seest put,
  It was for gentle Shakespeare cut:
Wherein the Graver had a strife
  with Nature, to out doo the life:
O, could he but have drawne his wit
  As well in brasse, as he hath hit
His face, the Print would then surpasse
  All, that was ever writ in brasse.
But, since he cannot, Reader, looke
  Not on his Picture, but his Booke.

Shakespeare died in Stratford in 1616, at the unbelievably early age of fifty-two.

II. SHAKESPEARE'S THEATRE

Shakespeare wrote most of his plays for the Globe Theatre. He wrote also for the Court, the Inns of Court, and, toward the end of his career, for the indoor stage of the Blackfriars' Theatre. But it was the Globe, its permanent acting-company, and its large public audiences, which chiefly determined the style of Shakespeare's dramaturgy. That theatre was Shakespeare's instrument, as important for his art as the orchestra available to a composer is for the music he writes.

Most of our knowledge of the Globe is derived from the contemporary sketch of the Swan—like the Globe, one of the "public theatres"—which is reproduced on the second page following. Recent students of Shakespeare's theatre have made far more elaborate, and largely conjectural, reconstructions of the Globe. (For three of the most valuable studies, see "Suggestions for Further Reading," below.) The following simplified description refers to the accompanying sketch.

In the center, the stage-house, where the actors dressed and stored their costumes and properties, rises to a height of three stories, and is topped by the "hut," where the flag flies. In front of it the platform (five or six feet above the ground) projects into the "yard" where the groundlings stood. The yard is encircled by three roofed balconies, and there the richer members of the audience sat on cushioned seats. The yard and part of the platform are open to the sky. The façade of the stage-house has large double doors on either side, and the Globe had also a central opening (not shown in the sketch) equipped with curtains which could be closed, or opened to reveal an inner room. There is a large balcony at the second-story level; and the hut could be used for musicians, sound effects, and machinery. A roof, called "the heavens," supported on tall, ornate pillars, covers the upper stage; and there was a trapdoor in the platform leading down to the cellar or "hell," which could also be entered from inside the stage-house.

This theatre may strike us as primitive, but Shakespeare's contemporaries thought it rich and splendid. The interior was elaborately carved and painted, in a style like that of the allegorical archways erected in the London streets for James the First's coronation. For performances the stage would be hung with banners and tapestries, or, for a tragedy, with black. The actors were gorgeously and expensively costumed, and they used elaborate properties, not only "hand-props" like weapons and torches, but portable thrones, altars, and the like. They made frequent use of sound effects for thunder or the noise of battle. Music, a widely cultivated art at the time, was important. In Shakespeare's plays it was an essential element of his theatrical "orchestration." He used it to change the mood, to stress a rhythm, or to punctuate the movement of the story.

The stage of the Globe, complicated as it was, was a permanent setting entirely unlike the modern "picture-frame" stage. Realistic or illusory settings of the kind we know were impossible, and the permanently visible structure could not be changed. The light came from the sky, and the resources of modern lighting were undreamed of. The effect was to focus attention upon the actors and what they said. The Globe could accommodate two thousand spectators or more, but packed closely around three sides of the stage, they could follow the subtleties of the playing

The Swan Theatre. Based on a drawing by Johannes de Witt in Arend van Buchell's commonplace book.

like audiences in our "arena" theatres. The audience looked, perforce, to the actors, not only to create the characters, but also to build imaginatively, in word and deed, the changing scenes of the story.

There is every reason to believe that the actors in Shakespeare's company were up to their great task. The arts of language both written and spoken were carefully cultivated, in the schools and pulpits as well as in the theatre. Actors were expected not only to command the language, but to dance, sing, play musical instruments, and fence well enough to please the connoisseurs. Women's parts were taken by boys, also highly trained. They had often been choristers, accustomed to singing good and difficult music, or members of one of the children's theatres. According to some contemporary testimony, they were better than the actresses on the continent. The art of acting, indeed—as distinguished from type-casting or the exploitation of the actor's sex or personality—was apparently well understood. The actors were used to playing a great variety of roles, often several parts in one production. The great Burbage played such varied characters as Hamlet, Macbeth, and Othello. Shakespeare himself must have chosen him for these roles, or written the roles for him, which strongly suggests that he was an artist with a very flexible and reliable technique. Shakespeare himself was an actor, and the art of acting is at the very root of his whole playwrighting art. We must think of that company, not like the cast of a Broadway show, hastily assembled for four weeks' rehearsal, but as resembling one of the highly trained companies of modern Europe. It must have been, in short, an accomplished and experienced ensemble.

Shakespeare's unrealistic or make-believe theatre, with the skilled player on the nearly empty platform, gave the dramatic poet great imaginative freedom. Modern playwrights often envy this freedom, and seek it on the arena-stage or on the bare stage. Thornton Wilder's *Our Town*, for instance, counts entirely on the actors and the willing audience to establish the scenes of the play. But Shakespeare's theatre, in its very structure, placed the poet and actors in the center, and so determined the style we know. In the opening scene of *Hamlet* Shakespeare, with the aid of two players, creates the night on the parapet in a matter of seconds:

BARNARDO: 'Tis now struck twelve, get thee to bed Francisco.
FRANCISCO: For this relief much thanks, 'tis bitter cold, And I am sick at heart.
BARNARDO: Have you had quiet guard?
FRANCISCO: Not a mouse stirring.

Much of the sweep of Shakespeare's poetry, its power to evoke scenes of many kinds and moods, is based on the collaboration between poet, actor, and audience in a theatre where literal realism was impossible.

On that stage, moreover, Shakespeare was not limited to a realistic time-scheme, or to detailed specifications of place. He used both time and place, not for documentation, but as means of conveying the action of the story. It is a mistake to inquire (as many students have felt obliged to do) just how many days or weeks Hamlet spent in England, or just which room in the palace Cleopatra occupies at the moment; such information is irrelevant to the unfolding of the play.

The stage of the Globe was, however, an extremely flexible instrument for suggesting changes of place where that was essential. The main playing-area was no doubt the platform, but the stage-house façade offered many other possibilities for the make-believe of the players. The big doors could be opened for the entrance of military processions, funerals, or royal progresses. The balcony could represent a castle-parapet, or Cleopatra's monument, or Juliet's bedroom window. The central opening might be used as an inner room, or its curtains might be suddenly opened to reveal a special effect, a prepared "set-piece" like the armed head, bloody child, and endless row of kings with which the Witches startle Macbeth. Careful studies of recent years have shown us how flexible that stage was. The clarity and theatrical effectiveness of Shakespeare's plays is evident as soon as one understands the stage for which he wrote them.

The traditional divisions of Shakespeare's plays into acts and scenes, with indications of place for every scene, were added by the long sequence of editors of the texts. The plays were originally played straight through, with no intermissions, and with only such suggestions of place as emerged from the play itself. The traditional labels of act, scene, and place are retained in this series to assist the reader (who does not have the benefit of Shakespeare's stage) to get his bearings. But to sense the rhythm which Shakespeare intended, one should think of the play as unfolding without a break from beginning to end.

One should also know something about what the theatre meant to Shakespeare's Londoners, for a theatre is partly the creation of its audience. The theatre was the Londoner's chief form of amusement, rivaled only by the bawdy-houses and the savage sport of bear-baiting. Everyone went to the theatre: the much-maligned groundlings who could stand in the yard and watch the show for a penny; law students, by all accounts a lively and intelligent group; the nobles and rich merchants, with their ladies; the " 'prentices," who have been described as clerks and young business people; in short, a cross-section of that great generation. They did not have our newspapers, magazines, movies, radio or television. Even books were much rarer and harder to get than they are now. The London theatre was a chief medium of public communication and an important instrument in the building of the common picture of man and his society. Holinshed and other more recent Chroniclers were interpreting English history as leading up to Elizabeth's beloved reign; Roman history, Italian and French fiction, and old stories and legends of many kinds, were widely read; and narratives from all these sources were made to live again in the performances of the players. Hamlet must have expressed the common feeling when he called the players "abstracts and brief chronicles of the time." His definition of the purpose of playing suggests what the theatre meant then: "To hold, as 'twere, the mirror up to nature; to show virtue her own feature, scorn her own image, and the very age and body of the time his form and pressure."

The proud device which Shakespeare's company adopted for their Globe Theatre was Hercules lifting the sphere of the earth. There are many indications in Shakespeare's plays that he thought of his theatre's "wooden O" as a microcosm, a symbolic representation of man's world as that age conceived it. Burbage, playing Hamlet, could point to the platform on which he stood as "this goodly frame, the earth," which seemed to him, in his melancholy, "a sterile premontory." When he spoke of the heavens as "this majestical roof fretted with golden fire" he had the actual roof far above his head, which was in fact painted, probably with stars, signs of the zodiac, or allegorical figures. When he heard his father's ghost the sound came from the cellerage or "hell" under the platform. Thus Shakespeare used his stage, not only to present the immediate events of the story, but also the cosmic setting where man, crawling between heaven and earth, met his mysterious fate. The modern reader can enter the world of Shakespeare's poetry more easily, and with fuller understanding, if he remembers that the symbolic stage itself was a basis for it.

III. SHAKESPEARE ON THE MODERN STAGE

The Puritan Revolution put an end to the theatre as Shakespeare had known it in 1642, when Parliament prohibited all stage-plays. The Restoration reopened the theatres in 1660, but the players had moved indoors, and most of the public theatres that Shakespeare used were gone. D'Avenant and Killigrew revived Shakespeare's plays at once, but Shakespeare would hardly have recognized them. The understanding of his art had decayed along with the theatres in which it was formed.

D'Avenant began the practice of adapting and "improving" Shakespeare for the new theatre. He arranged the plays for the indoor stages of Restoration London, which were already beginning to resemble our proscenium-stages, dividing them into scenes which could be realistically or spectacularly set. He also drastically altered the texts to suit the taste of the new society. He cut or re-wrote passages which he found indelicate; he re-arranged plots to make them "clearer" or more moral; and he was quite willing to shift whole scenes from one play to another. Many of his bad habits governed the staging of Shakespeare almost to our own day. The barnstorming Shakespeareans whom our grandfathers saw in opera-houses all over this country were essentially within that tradition.

It was Granville-Barker, after William Poel, who did the most to free the staging of Shakespeare from its inherited encumbrances. He demonstrated in his own productions and in his famous *Prefaces to Shakespeare* that the plays—including those which had been thought literary and unstageable—are extraordinarily clear and effective in the theatre, provided the director does not feel obliged to pause and set a realistic scene with every change of place. As the implications of Granville-Barker's views were worked out, the flexibility and imaginative scope of Shakespeare's stage-techniques became clearer and clearer to a new generation in the theatre.

Contemporary producers inherit this improved understanding of Shakespeare's purely theatrical effectiveness. There is no longer any need to think that Shakespeare is hard to stage simply because realistic staging strangles him. Moreover our theatre is no longer limited to realism or heavy romantic spectacle. We are accustomed to permanent settings, arenas, bare stages, and other arrangements designed to secure for poet and performer the kind of freedom Shakespeare enjoyed. The modern producer is in a good position to understand Shakespeare's theatrical intentions, and he is free, after that, to consult his own taste—subject, of course, to the limitations imposed by his budget, his actors, and his audience.

If no standard form of Shakespeare-staging has emerged in our time, that is because the theatre itself is so varied. The productions we see, good and bad in different ways, reflect a bewildering variety of intentions. Modern dress may be used to stress the contemporaneity of a play like *Troilus;* productions like Copeau's use period music and costume for poetic purposes; *Coriolanus* or *Julius Caesar* may be pointed up in such a way as to bring out a fascist (or anti-fascist) thesis. Shakespeare is constantly adapted to the movies, television, radio, and dance and opera. In recent years off-Broadway, college, and community theatres have often staged Shakespeare "straight"—relying on the acting and directing, and spending very little on sets and costumes. Some of these productions have had great vitality and unexpected but convincing subtlety; probably they give the best sense of Shakespeare's own direct theatrical style.

There is room in our time for many interpretations of Shakespeare, both on and off the stage. The comments on separate plays in this series, written by well-known actors, directors, poets, and critics, are intended to suggest some of the living approaches to Shakespeare, and some of the meanings which his many-sided art has for us.

SUGGESTIONS FOR FURTHER READING

This short list is intended to assist the reader who wishes to inform himself further about Shakespeare in the light of modern studies. Most of the books referred to are easy to find in libraries or recent editions. Asterisks (*) indicate books available in paperbound editions.

Many of the books listed below contain bibliographies, and more detailed studies of particular plays are listed in the Introductions to this series.

I. SHAKESPEARE'S LIFE AND TIMES

*Chute, Marchette. *Shakespeare of London.* New York: 1956.

    An excellent popular biography, containing the known facts without the usual uncertain speculations. Especially valuable for its careful accounts of Stratford, London, Shakespeare's theatres, and his colleagues and patrons.

Halliday, F. E. *Shakespeare: A Pictorial Biography*. New York: 1956.
A short account of the known facts of Shakespeare's life and surroundings, profusely illustrated with photographs, prints, and other pictorial materials.

*Trevelyan, G. M. *History of England*. Volume II: The Tudors and the Stuart Era. New York: 1953.
A short and readable account of English history in the time of Shakespeare.

*Tillyard, E. M. W. *The Elizabethan World Picture*. New York: 1944.
A description of the way man, his society, and his world looked in Shakespeare's time. It throws light on Shakespeare's theatre, which was a kind of model of the Elizabethan's "world," and on the background of his poetry.

*Fluchère, Henri. *Shakespeare and the Elizabethans*, with a Foreword by T. S. Eliot. New York: 1956.
A recent and stimulating book on Shakespeare the dramatist, in relation to other Elizabethans, and to the times in which they lived.

*Eliot, T. S. *Essays on Elizabethan Drama*. New York: 1956.
Brief essays which do not include Shakespeare, but the book is one of the most influential of recent years, and clearly illustrates the new interest in the poetry and drama of Shakespeare's age.

II. SHAKESPEARE IN THE THEATRE

Adams, John Cranford. *The Globe Playhouse: Its Design and Equipment*. New York: 1942.

Hodges, C. Walter. *The Globe Restored*. New York: 1954.

Smith, Irwin. *Shakespeare's Globe Playhouse. A Modern Reconstruction in Text and Scale Drawings*. New York: 1956.

> Dr. Adams's book is the most elaborate recent effort to reconstruct Shakespeare's own theatre. It is based on painstaking scholarship, but many details are necessarily conjectural, and are questioned by other authorities. The other two books rely very much on Dr. Adams's, but differ in details. Mr. Smith is interested in the methods of actual construction in Shakespeare's time. Mr. Hodges' study is the shortest and most readable, and contains many well-chosen illustrations.

*Granville-Barker, Harley. *Prefaces to Shakespeare*. Princeton: 1946.

> The fundamental book on Shakespeare's plays as works for the theatre. Ten plays are discussed from the point of view of their staging as Shakespeare himself planned it. Granville-Barker was both an authority on Shakespeare's stage and a skilled director in the modern theatre.

De Banke, Cecile. *Shakespearean Production, Then and Now. A Manual for the Scholar Player*. New York: 1953.

*Watkins, Ronald. *On Producing Shakespeare*. London: 1950.

*Webster, Margaret. *Shakespeare without Tears*. New York: 1957.

> These three books are concerned with the modern staging of Shakespeare. Professor De Banke's is addressed primarily to the school or college director. Mr. Watkins is talking to professionals, and arguing for the necessity of understanding Shakespeare's own theatre-practice. Miss Webster speaks out of her wide experience as a producer of Shakespeare here and in England. Her book is useful also for those who wish only to read the plays.

III. CRITICISM AND INTERPRETATION

*Bradley, A. C. *Shakespearean Tragedy*. New York: 1955.

Bradley summarizes the best nineteenth century criticism, which emphasizes the creation of character. His book is one of the foundations for the modern understanding of Shakespeare. This volume is concerned primarily with *Hamlet, Othello, King Lear,* and *Macbeth*.

Coleridge's Writings on Shakespeare. Terence Hawks, editor. New York: 1959.

A convenient collection of Coleridge's writings and lectures on Shakespeare, arranged according to topics and the plays.

*Goddard, Harold C. *The Meaning of Shakespeare*. Chicago: 1950.

A stimulating reading of all of Shakespeare; a useful and provocative introduction.

Samuel Johnson on Shakespeare. W. K. Wimsatt, Jr., editor. New York: 1960.

A useful collection of Dr. Johnson's trenchant comments on Shakespeare's works.

*Traversi, D. A. *An Approach to Shakespeare*. New York: 1956.

A short study by a well-known English critic who has taken account of recent developments in Shakespeare criticism.

*Van Doren, Mark. *Shakespeare*. New York: 1953.

A reading of all of Shakespeare's works by a scholar who is also a sensitive lyric poet.

*Clemen, W. H. *The Development of Shakespeare's Imagery*. Cambridge, Mass.: 1951.

*Moulton, R. G. *Shakespeare as Dramatic Artist*. Oxford: 1929.

These two books, which are somewhat technical, are concerned with Shakespeare's art as a writer of plays. Clemen's book may serve as an introduction to the many recent studies of Shakespeare's poetry. Moulton's is still the best analysis of Shakespeare's methods in constructing his plots.

Shakespeare Criticism: A Selection. D. N. Smith, editor. Oxford: 1916.
Shakespeare Criticism, 1919-1935. Selected with an Introduction by Anne Bradby. Oxford: 1936.
*Shakespeare, Modern Essays in Criticism. Leonard F. Dean, editor. New York: 1957.
> These three books constitute a useful sampling of the vast literature of Shakespeare criticism from his own time to ours.

IV. REFERENCE BOOKS

The New Variorum Shakespeare. H. H. Furness and H. H. Furness, editors. Philadelphia: 1878—.
> Most of Shakespeare's more important plays have appeared in this series, which is being continued by a committee of the Modern Language Association. It contains exhaustive notes on textual problems, many critical comments, and some sources.

The First Folio of Shakespeare's Plays, in a Facsimile Edition. Helge Kokeritz and Charles Tyler Prouty, editors. New Haven: 1955.
> The facsimile of the First Folio, published originally by Shakespeare's colleagues, is harder to read than a modern edition; but the old spelling and punctuation give valuable insights into Shakespeare's language.

Sisson, C. J. *New Readings in Shakespeare.* Two Vols. Cambridge: 1956.
> The latest authoritative survey of the problems of Shakespeare's text, with an illuminating essay on modern methods of textual analysis, by the textual editor of this series.

A Shakespeare Glossary. C. T. Onions, editor. Oxford: 1919.
A New and Complete Concordance or Verbal Index to Words, Phrases, and Passages in the Dramatic Works of Shakespeare. John Bartlett, compiler. New York: 1894.
Chambers, E. K. *The Elizabethan Stage.* Four Vols. Oxford: 1923.

Chambers, E. K. *William Shakespeare: A Study of Facts and Problems.* Oxford: 1930.

> The two works of Chambers are a mine of information, and the foundation of a great deal of modern Shakespeare scholarship.

*Bentley, G. E. *Shakespeare, A Biographical Handbook.* New Haven: 1961.

> A readable account of all the certain sources for Shakespeare's biography.

Bentley, G. E. *The Jacobean and Caroline Stage.* Five Vols. Oxford: 1941-56.

> This is the standard work on the English stage. It carries Chambers' work, which ends with the death of Shakespeare, to the closing of the theatres. Volumes I and II are devoted to "Dramatic Companies and Players," Volumes III, IV, and V to "Plays and Playwrights."

Shakespeare's England: An Account of the Life and Manners of His Age. Two Vols. Oxford: 1916.

> A collection of essays by experts in various fields, planned by the late Sir Walter Raleigh. Very useful as background for the plays.

Ralli, Augustus. *A History of Shakespeare Criticism.* Two Vols. Oxford: 1932.

Odell, George C. D. *Shakespeare from Betterton to Irving.* Two Vols. New York: 1920.

> A history of Shakespeare productions since the Restoration.

A Companion to Shakespeare Studies. Harley Granville-Barker and G. B. Harrison, editors. New York: 1934.

> Essays by leading authorities on Shakespeare's life, theatre, poetry, and sources, and on scholarly and critical problems. Useful in itself and as a guide to further study.

Ebisch, Walther, and Schucking, L. L. *A Shakespeare Bibliography.* Oxford: 1931.

────── Supplement for the Years 1930-1935. Oxford: 1937.

Glossary Notes

This glossary, based on the glossary prepared by Hilda Hulme for the *Complete Works of Shakespeare* edited by C. J. Sisson, was made especially for *Henry the Eighth* by Lawrence Blonquist. Unfamiliar words, names, foreign phrases, and English words used in unfamiliar senses are defined here. Words which may easily be found in any standard modern dictionary are generally not included.

aboded: foretold.
advised: cautious.
affect: to display for effect.
ague: cold fits of fever.
an: if.
Andren: probably Ardennes, a small province in northern France, bordering Belgium.
anon: soon.
appliance: medicine.
Arde: Ardes, small village in Puy-de-Dôme province, in south central France.
attach: to take possession of.
attainder: disgrace.
attend: to wait.
avaunt: exclamation of contempt.
(to give): (to send away).

beadle: public whipper.
beholding: obliged.
beshrew me: indeed.
Bevis: fabulous hero in the time of William the Conqueror.
bore: to pierce.
brake: thicket.
broken: interrupted.

carders: gamblers.
Carnarvonshire: county in Wales.
cast: to throw away.
certes: certainly.
chalk: to mark, trace out.
chamblet: camlet: a costly satin fabric, woven from camel's hair or angora

wool; *camelot:* any cheap merchandise; peddler of cheap merchandise.
cheveril: soft leather; symbol of pliant flexibility.
chine: a piece of the spine cut for cooking.
choler: anger.
Cinque-ports: five English harbors lying toward France; they were permitted to send two men to Parliament in return for furnishing ships of war.
cliquant: glittering.
Clotharius: French King of Merovingian dynasty.
colt's tooth: youthful wantonness.
congee: to bow.
content: contentment.
conjunction: union, connection.
construction: interpretation.
cum privilegio: with rights, advantage.

Daring th' event to th' teeth: taking great risks, going "all the way."
device: plot, scheme.
discourser: observer, narrator.

effect: to bring about.
Ego et Rex Meus: I and My King.
element: proper or natural sphere; he would be expected to "feel at home" in such a business.
envious: malignant, spiteful.
exhalation: bright phenomenon, meteor.

fain: gladly.
Faith: indeed.
file: catalogue.
flawed: cracked, broken.
front: to stand in front.
fuller: tradesman who cleans cloth.

gripe: to seize, grasp.
Guines: a small village in the northern French province Pas-de-Calais.

halberd: battle-axe fixed to a long pole.
hap: fortune.
holidam (halidom): blessedness; used in swearing.
husband: one who is careful and economical.

in's: in his.
Indies: source of spices, cloth, jewels, etc.; symbol of paradise.
Ipswich: Wolsey's birthplace.

keech: fat of a slaughtered animal rolled into a bundle; name of Wolsey, the

Glossary Notes

butcher's son, as also of his wife.
knock (music k. it): to strike ("it" is superfluous).

league: friendship, truce.
Limbus Patrum: Limbo of the Fathers; place where the Saints of the Old Testament remained until Christ's descent into Hell.
Limehouse: an unknown locality in London (an unexplained passage).
look: expression, countenance.

manor: an estate.
Marshalsea: a prison.
mettle: courage, spirit of enterprise.
moiety: half.

niggard: miser.

pale: (an unclear passage; a possible mistake for "pate").
Pepin: founder of the Carolingian dynasty.
period: goal.
phoenix: a bird who, every 500 years, dies in flames only to be reborn from its own ashes.
physic: medicine.
porringer: a dish for broth; a cap which is shaped like a porringer.
Powle's (Paul's): St. Paul's Church; the principal cathedral of London.
practice: plot.
praemunire: a writ issued against one who has committed the offense of introducing a foreign authority or power into England.
presence: state-room.
pride: magnificence, splendid adornment.
primero: card game.
privity: joint knowledge.
propped: supported.

Saba: Queen of Sheba.
sacring bell: bell rung at Mass.
salute: to touch, affect.
showed: appeared.
sickened: weakened, suffered losses.
spanned: measured-out.
spavin: disease of horses; lameness from swollen joints.
spoons: a common present given by sponsors at a christening.
spring halt: disease of horses causing itching and lameness.
stick: to hesitate.
sufferance: pain, torment.

Tanta est erga te mentis integritas, Regina serenissima: Such is the integrity of mind towards you, most illustrious Queen.

Te Deum: the first words of a well-known anonymous Latin hymn: Te Deum Laudamus—We Praise Thee Our God.

tell: to count.

tender: to offer.

Tower Hill: meeting place of the Puritans in Shakespeare's day.

tract: description, course.

traduce: to blame, censure.

trow: believe.

viva voce: in live voice; alive and in person.

vouch: assertion, testimony.

worship: dignity, authority.

wot: to know.

A NOTE ON THE GENERAL EDITOR

After completing three years at Oxford on a Rhodes Scholarship, Francis Fergusson was Assistant Director of the American Laboratory Theatre for four years. He has taught at the New School for Social Research, Bennington College, and Indiana University, was a member of the Institute for Advanced Study at Princeton University, and director of the Princeton Seminars in Literary Criticism. He is now University Professor of Comparative Literature at Rutgers. Professor Fergusson is the author of The Idea of a Theatre, Dante's Drama of the Mind, *and* The Human Image in Dramatic Literature.

A NOTE ON THE TYPE AND LAYOUT

The Laurel Shakespeare is composed in Times Roman, an unusually clear and readable type face. Its qualities of compactness make possible a larger size of type than that used in most editions of Shakespeare past and present. The text of the plays has been arranged with the names of the speakers on separate lines; this is the arrangement generally used in the professional theatre for acting scripts as well as reading versions. The line numbers of The Laurel Shakespeare are those of the Globe Edition of 1864; these line numbers are the ones used for reference by almost all Shakespearean critics.

THE LAUREL SHAKESPEARE SERIES
General Editor, Francis Fergusson

ALL'S WELL THAT ENDS WELL 45c
ANTONY AND CLEOPATRA 40c
AS YOU LIKE IT 35c
THE COMEDY OF ERRORS 35c
CORIOLANUS 35c
CYMBELINE 45c
HAMLET 40c
HENRY IV, PART I 35c
HENRY IV, PART II 35c
HENRY V 35c
HENRY VI, PARTS I, II, and III 95c
JULIUS CAESAR 35c
KING JOHN 35c
KING LEAR 40c
LOVE'S LABOUR'S LOST 35c
MACBETH 40c
MEASURE FOR MEASURE 35c
THE MERCHANT OF VENICE 35c
THE MERRY WIVES OF WINDSOR 45c
A MIDSUMMER NIGHT'S DREAM 35c
MUCH ADO ABOUT NOTHING 35c
OTHELLO 40c
PERICLES 50c
RICHARD II 35c
RICHARD III 35c
ROMEO AND JULIET 35c
THE TAMING OF THE SHREW 35c
THE TEMPEST 45c
TIMON OF ATHENS 35c
TROILUS AND CRESSIDA 50c
TWELFTH NIGHT 45c
THE TWO GENTLEMEN OF VERONA 35c
THE WINTER'S TALE 35c
SONNETS 35c
NARRATIVE POETRY OF SHAKESPEARE 75c
—M. K. Spears Ed.

In addition to the play, each volume contains a glossary, an introduction by the general editor, a commentary by an eminent Shakespearean actor, director, or critic, and an account of Shakespeare's life and dramatic career.

If you cannot obtain copies of these titles at your local bookstore, just send the price (plus 10c per copy for handling and postage) to Dell Books, Box 2291, Grand Central Post Office, New York, N.Y. 10017. No postage or handling charge is required on any order of five or more books.